AF616626

Also by Philip Fried

MUTUAL TRESPASSES (Ion, 1988)

QUANTUM GENESIS (Zohar, 1997)

BIG MEN SPEAKING TO LITTLE MEN (Salmon, 2006)

COHORT (Salmon, 2009)

ACQUAINTED WITH THE NIGHT (Rizzoli, 1997)

(With Lynn Saville), Editor

Early/Late

New & Selected Poems

PHILIP FRIED

salmonpoetry

Published in 2011 by
Salmon Poetry
Cliffs of Moher, County Clare, Ireland
Website: www.salmonpoetry.com
Email: info@salmonpoetry.com

ISBN 978-1-907056-57-4

Cover photograph: "*Girl on Highline" by Lynn Saville*
Cover design & typesetting: *Siobhán Hutson*
Printed by imprint*digital*.net

For Mollie and Lynn

Contents

from MUTUAL TRESPASSES

from QUANTUM GENESIS

from Big Men Speaking to Little Men

New Poems:
The Emanation Crunch

"Money is a kind of poetry."

—Wallace Stevens

"… the exuberant world of It.*"*

—Martin Buber

Bits

And the world's great markets, trading floors strewn with shouts and confetti, diminished to circuitry. Digital impulses, bits. All the nations' economies now the size of an acorn, lying in the palm of a hand. Plump acorn. All monies in miniature.

And we seek rest in this thing that is everything, but so little, where no rest is. And we know not our God, which is confidence regained that will stabilize, loosen, and reassure. Which is the heavenly treasury, central of centrals, conferring courage to invest and lend. Heartbeat in the eternal circulation of credit.

But now, I behold the head bleeding, insolvency in the doleful sessions, and points that are continually shed. For our sins of greed he died. And ascended above the indices to the heavens of all the profits, but will soon return to make intercession in our behalf, driving out devils of volatility. And nothing but faith in faith itself will deliver us from lurches, panic, and slide.

But I could not believe the world's vast systems and risks were contained in this kernel, the mighty but finite quantities bound for the infinitesimal infinity. Adventure that was scarcely a compensation for the fading pageant. Now, the frantic trading but ever diminishing, cries and curses at the atomic verge.

Father They Value as the Dawn

One morning, traveling and never arriving, although the commute is clocked and foreordained, Eternity of every instant.

In the meager span between thumb and forefinger, as they grip a few sheets of wide paper, the dream unfolds.

Fingers remember father's shoulder, under the weave of a shirt, the strength and weakness of that boney curve. Shoulder that cushioned the blow of crisis.

A single sleeper is lying, muttering and moaning, on the uneven, rocky ground of the story. And cannot awake to the Father they value as the dawn.

The crowd sway and lightly graze shoulders as windows rush by in darkness, in light. Panic Boulevard, Turmoil Plaza, Faltering Bridge, all the stations.

And the dreamer gasps as the story holds its breath to continue, pages later. The news stains fingerprints with forced selling.

As they hurtle and stand, eyes wary or inward, there are many places to which they are fleeing, though there is no one even pursuing.

The dream zooms in on a see-sawing tot, as the sleeper, creased with deterioration, exhales in a silent voice, "Each day we are walking on shaky ground."

Celestial, Inc.

I regret to inform you that, in the purview of immutable discretion, it has now become necessary to downsize the elect.

It may seem strange that of the great body of humankind some like yourself, predestined to salvation, should be laid off.

But please bear in mind that the Boss does not guarantee for all an eternal position, and even those initially receiving the wages of grace may be let go.

It must be plain how greatly ignorance of this principle detracts from His glory and impairs true humility.

In your pre-termination meeting, you will be briefed on re-salvation options. You may come as a grievant or a supplicant.

Now, quickly step away from your papers, even those with only stray marks and doodles, and a guard will escort you from the Office.

If you have any question about how your severance reveals the obscurity of the Boss's say-so, don't hesitate to contact me.

Thank you for the services you have rendered, and I wish you every success in your post-salvation existence.

Offering

We, the Partnership, exclusive agents for the Boundless One, reveal in this confidential memorandum the great abundance that is hidden.

We disclose this knowledge solely to you who dwell in the poverty of yourself, nor may this offering be reproduced or used for another purpose.

The Partnership will act as a master fund for Imperishable Limited, an off-Earth company formed eons ago for converting dust-filled chaos to pure fire.

For you, trapped in this middling region of meager returns, the Partnership offers a chance to reinvest your dole of dimness in the exalted infinite Light.

To facilitate such salvation, the Partnership engages in supernal arbitrage, offsetting a put for the suffering body with a call for the ineffable spirit.

This strategy enables investors to participate simultaneously in rising and falling markets, converting the gall of regulation to the honey of opportunity.

In expectation of a growing perpetuity, the Partnership bestows on the General Partner, Hermes T. Megistus, ultimate responsibility for investment decisions.

The law insists that we allude to the risk of speculation, but as your companions in the Totality, we urge you to parlay your soul into Logos with our leveraged portfolio.

The Emanation Crunch

Lawyers in Pleroma & Pleroma, a restructuring and insolvency practice, are expert in every aspect of redemption and spiritual bankruptcy work.

The practice advises individuals and institutions alike, all that have suffered from the Lucre's compulsion to clone itself through derivative vehicles with proliferating names.

Recent turmoil in the realm of dispersal has induced the formal insolvency of ever more complicated entities and undermined a perfect faith in credit, which is the flow of life eternal based on a firm knowledge of the Totalities.

Mastering this divided and disturbed environment, lawyers in the practice have been extensively involved in workouts like these:

Acting for the Receivers of Exaltation and Abundance Limited, a Structured Investment Vehicle funded by commercial manifestations of the Father.

Advising the proposed Master Fluidity Enhancement Conduit (superfund) designed to alleviate the impact of the emanation crunch.

In this multi-jurisdictional middle region, this maze of receiverships, liquidations, and arrangements, the practice will cavil and controvert on your behalf, will safeguard the stake that eases retirement into redemption, the entrance into what is silent.

Ballade (of the Brands of Future Times)

for Jon Jorgensen

Tell me where, or in what domain,
Are *Serente*, a serious but seductive name
With peaceful and enlightened overtones
To sell derivatives or package loans;
Diamia, "my day," to celebrate
A unique someone or a special date;
And playful *Cycliq* for what spins in cycles.
Where is the imminent blizzard of brandable names?

Where is *Aphora*, whose classical pedigree
Offers the burnish and aura of History,
Especially for a brick-and-mortar business
That seeks to expand into cyber space?
But if *Aphora*'s hint of euphoria
Is over the line, where is *Amolia*,
Fluid-sounding yet gentle and multilingual?
Where is the imminent blizzard of brandable names?

Olixo, oh so short but memorable;
Long vowels emotional while "x" is stable.
Ethair, fresh and green and lighter than air,
With minimal carbon footprint. No polluter.
Then, for fiscal services, lovely *Xillio*,
Sure to multiply millions into zillions.
Or if you're musty, *Cacheup* would lisp "technology."
Where is the imminent blizzard of brandable names?

Investor, don't beg me for *Bigabite* or *Adflair*.
I cannot access limbo's database,
And my roll-call of *noms fatals* is over:
Where is the imminent blizzard of brandable names?

Heavenly Enterprises

Business traveler, you must have heard of the affordable bliss of Hotel Paradise, and of the life of our first parents there, and of the debt they still incurred, about which so many have written.

Heavenly Enterprises is dedicated to restoring that bliss, and little has been lost in the interim: Almost every extinct species, from the auk to t. rex, is a virtual guest in the gardens of our theme-park resorts.

Sound tracks replay, in loops, the hypothetical hoots and growls associated with numerous fossils, micro or macro, and travelers with a laptop can rename the species by playing our world-famous Adam Game.

A daily "Indulge Your Vanity" schedule on TV shows times for every activity: today, for instance, in ten-min. intervals, gathering then casting away stones in the garden, followed by weeping and laughing at the bar.

No need for a Gideon in a drawer when room service—run by the Four Prophets, Izzy, Jerry, Zeke, and Mike, with offices on-site—will send a mock-harangue deliverer to your door, 24/7.

In every room, remote controls can prompt hologram reenactments of parables: an almost-actual camel passes through a real needle's eye or like a summoned bell-hop, the returning prodigal sieves through your door.

And last but far from least, *Revelations of the Apocalypse* is available for adult viewing and for a minimal fee can be watched with special 3d glasses that make the Whore of Babylon pop.

Admired but not easily replicated, the Heavenly nimbus (see our logo) truly glows around our employees — personnel who share a single focus and are inspired to offer unparalleled sacrifices.

Multi-tasker with a mobile portal, by grace a stranger with business in this world, and by grace a Predestined Heavenly Guest, prosper and claim your pre-selected status. Rest in the one irrevocable choice.

Pansophical Ltd.

In business, as in life, all success comes as a blessing from the Boss of the universe, a CEO who is not the figurehead of a slumbering omnipotence, but a vigilant and ever-active executive.

Do not defraud the Boss of his glory. Access his providential algorithms, especially in this time of adversity, by downloading our Pansophical-Trader Software.

Pansophical robotically monitors the market second by second, numbering every hair of fiscal variance. Programmed to skim the milk-and-honey securities, it executes your orders automatically.

Supernally logical, Pansophical cannot panic-buy or -sell. It "sees" market conditions invisible to a mortal, marking the fall of stocks as small as Sparrow Co.

Pansophical provides a sim-world for testing trades in a virtual dust-to-dust environment. With just one wizard click, you can switch between the Simulator and Live Modes.

By accessing posts to the Destiny Message-Board, our subscribers out-vie sluggish rivals, darting in and out of the market as fast as the pros.

No affiliation is needed, and software is free with subscription activation. No broker will stand between Providence and your program as you run sample-hereafters in the real-time simulator.

To conclude with a retiree's testimonial, "The Boss himself was the first Pansophical Trader, accumulating futures in creatures and souls when there were only markets in void and darkness."

Be *Then*—Now!™

They've rolled out software that can parse your memory,
tag the players blooming into imagoes,
and foreground them in immersive imagery.
"Conversion technology was the *sine qua non*
for our company," says CEO N.O. Syne.
"We're churning out 3D retrofits." Data collection
from clients leaving the theaters of their minds
revealed that if money is spent and time taken,
the enhancement of recollection is impeccable:
Music executive Lauren Shotwell attested
her upgraded memory betrayed no tell-tale
signs of conversion, like ghosting or blurriness;
Fee Nix, nail technician, proclaimed his own past
was "finally on a par with *Avatar*."

Prospectus

Customized Low-cost Incarceration (CLINC)

In this time of job loss and financial stress, CLINC is committed to providing government partners with no less than world-class correctional services.

Since the company's founding in 1980, CLINC has continued to lead the private correction industry, not only in experience, but in quality, design, and security.

Five Qualities of Incarceration Excellence—admired in the industry but never successfully emulated—set CLINC apart in the minds of elected officials and specialists:

Proficiency: In evidence of its long-term commitment, CLINC has secured a corrections management team with a seven-centuries' record of criminal justice service.

Execution: CLINC's amazingly low escape rates from high-security facilities outstrip those in the public sector by .16 inmates, per data from the *Corrections Yearbook.*

Adaptability: Like fingerprints, no two correctional systems are identical, and CLINC's vast scale enables partners to address fluctuating bed needs with customized contracts.

Community: Outreach is the key to our success, and we rely on interlocking committees—wardens, civic leaders, and media executives—to loop in our neighboring communities.

Efficiency: Our per-diem rates are the envy of the industry, and our classic dormitory wing, with large capacity for little outlay, is a model for affordable public housing.

When the forensic chalk lines imply any body and a guilty world, we ease the distress with economies of scale. Our corporate mission is to safeguard more and more for less, in the correctional universe.

Following Him on Twitter

A man or a woman, afraid with any sudden
chance of fire or of man's death is driven
to cry or to pray after help. Yea, how?

•

Surely, not in many words, nor yet
in one word of two syllables. And therefore
he cryeth a little word: as "fire!" or "out!"

•

For in ghostliness all is one, height and deepness,
and rather it pierceth my "ears" than any
long psalter unmindfully mumbled in the teeth.

•

Then feel sin a lump, thou wottest never what,
but only thyself. And cry then ghostly
ever on one: "a Sin, sin, sin! Out, out, out!"

God-fearing

He's the catastrophe we strive to cap
with ice-like hydrates, blowout preventer stacks.
Gushing spill in a world of scarcity.
Hemorrhage of energy, despite every
tourniquet of containment. Infinite spew.
Staunchless plume of animacules, the nimble
swimmers jostling in any cubic centimeter.
Plenty's horn, the topsy-turvy tornado.

We are engineers, contriving options,
tapping and funneling, drilling counter wells
that will never arrive at the infant Omnipotence
who rock-a-byes inside us, the purler that broke
the goat's horn.
North is stretched out over the empty
place. Earth hangs upon Nothing. Myth is irrevocable.

From the Mortality Desk

DEBRIS is a full-service credit rating agency, unaffiliated, privately held, adhering only to free-market gospel.

Our creed: that unfettered capital will redeem us from sub-prime abominations and previous sins of securitization.

Our mission: to work as instruments of financial faith by restoring credible options for the global marketplace.

Per this quest, the analysts at our Mortality Desk will rate an ingenious new death-based derivative.

By grace of a win-win transaction, life-policies cashed in by the ill and elderly are bundled in tranches for a death payout.

Pundits concur with DEBRIS on this bond's redemptive merit—bets on timely death are free of stocks' volatility.

However, to reap the promise of this novel field, we needed to hone the old mortality models.

Countering the threat of long life, the Methuselah Liability, we performed statistical smoothing for the over-healthy.

Then, factoring in the stress of medical progress, we filtered out clusters of cancer to forestall the "cure" risk.

The resulting table, rule-based and formulaic, will gauge the justified yield on decease.

As this market matures, DEBRIS will monitor every advance, in curing disease or chance, that impacts belief in the deal.

Amicus Curiae

We of the Alias Guild hereby proclaim our identity and interest in the lawsuit brought by Simpkin-Simon against the Authentication Board for deceased artist Arriba Ditto.

In addressing this rehearing *en banc*, we designate ourselves a diffuse association of studio groups, each working to produce the *oeuvre* of a famous artistic name.

As the court well knows, Simpkin-Simon's suit alleges that the board routinely withholds its imprimatur from legitimate Dittos to sharply limit the total of Dittos on the market.

It is further alleged that, as duplicitous executors of the Ditto estate, the board has one sole reason for this ruse—to boost the worth of its own Ditto hoard.

Exempli gratia, regarding the 1965 *Nonself Nonportraits*, the board is driven to the farcical admission that these works "are not *by* Arriba Ditto, though signed, dedicated, and dated by same Ditto."

Ergo, the board omits the pivotal point that it is Ditto's very nonparticipation in producing the images, a noninvolvement imbued with glamour and humor, that renders them authentic.

Was the board unaware that the lodestar of Ditto's career was his fascination with the "Copy," coupled with his nonchalant debunking of the myth of the auteur, the sole and solitary fount of art?

Or that, only weeks before the subcontracting of the silk-screened *Nonself*, Ditto had offhandedly observed to an interviewer from the glossy *Haut Bas*, "I am becoming a factory"?

Or further that, as philosopher Ned Inkling elucidated in his *Meditation on Ditto,* "The question he poses is not, 'to be or not to be,' but the far more acute, 'how to be *and* not be'?

". . . And its compelling corollary, with fiscal consequences for Western thought, 'Is profit the only difference between identical objects, one of which is art and one not?'"

Hence the Alias Guild respectfully seconds Simpkin-Simon's claim, noting that if you find in his favor, we unseen makers will teem under the aegis of eminent signatures. *E pluribus unum.*

A Chorus Line

SUN
What do you think it takes to succeed in this game?
Performance is deception. To subdue
the "enemy" by hardly moving — every
little step a thrilling combination —
is the acme of skill. Be extremely
subtle, to the point of formlessness;
mysterious, to the point of soundlessness.

VON
Performance is danger, physical effort, uncertainty.
Play me the music, give me the tumult, the mirror,
help me to prove I'm strong, give me the music,
a place to maneuver, a cause in which to believe.
Get me involved and the rest of the crap will get solved.
Kick — kick — kick — kick — kick —
war is song and dance by other means.

LEE and ULY
Remember our duet in Appomattox?
The courthouse scene. How could I forget?
The sweetness and the sorrow. Wish me luck.
The same to you. But how can I regret
what I did for love. My eyes are dry.
The gift was ours to borrow. We always knew
and won't forget, what we did for love.

MAC
I've slayed them before in the best-known shows and I shall
return for more. They loved me in Luzon,
they all claimed I brought down the house in Tokyo Bay,
and they raved about my amphibious moves in Incheon.
But what does he want from me now? Who should I be?
So many faces around and here we go.
I can't just fade, Oh God, I need this show.

CRYSTAL
Hits and assets, got myself the pair,
then tightened up my flank and derrière.
Just a little surge, didn't cost a fortune,
just a dash of "military silicone."
With hits and assets, hearings are a litany
of "sweetie genius, darling of the nation."
I smile demurely, flaunt my augmentation.

PET
One smile and suddenly nobody else will do,
or so they say. One singular sensation,
every little step I take, it's often
noted. Nor do I really have to mention
the discipline that propels me through auditions
or my leap, step, kick, the flick and follow through
as I clear and hold the stage, and steal their show.

Statement

Good afternoon, you may wonder why these forty
folding chairs are set out upon the mountain of Zion,
which is so desolate the foxes walk upon it.

Years ago, I was unfaithful to my wife, my family,
my team. Now I am stripped bare,
and the city of me sits solitary.

With my family at my side, I apologize
to anybody viewing this broadcast. Behold
if there is any sorrow like mine.

For these *things* I weep; mine eye
runneth down with water . . . my children are desolate,
Marshall, Bolton, Landon, and Blake.

I let them down by creating a fiction.
It began very innocently with just a casual e-mail,
but He hath broken my teeth with gravel stones.

It's the same old thing again. Adulation,
admiration, then a stress fracture of the left heel.
My flesh and my skin He hath made old; He hath broken my bones.

Now the rampart and the wall lament; they languish together.
I wish I had never played in those ballparks
during the steroid era.

The bottom line: God's law is not a rigid, moral
list of dos and don'ts for the heck of it
but is designed to protect

us from the biggest self of self.
Now my neck is under persecution . . .
Reporters sitting down and soon rising up,

I am their music.
The media thrusts its microphone into the dust
and transmits into the ionosphere

so anyone can bookmark this apology.
I alone am responsible.
I will not be taking questions.

Karaoke

> *. . . Einstein's treatment of this concept has a noteworthy prehistory that can be traced back to antiquity.*
>
> —Max Jammer, *Concepts of Simultaneity*

I sing the Now, although it so worried Einstein,
The Now of you everywhere
Hearing me croon this nightshade valediction:
I did it my way.

Amid the lightnings and thunderings and voices,
I intone a flinty anthem:
Regrets I've had a few, too few to mention,
Doubts, I spat them out.

Yes, it's true, from Parmenides to Hawking,
I've had my share of losing,
But I've heard the doo-wop at the globe's four corners:
Doing it my way, yeah.

Zeno was a fan of paradox.
He loved and laughed and cried,
Said everything but Being was absurd,
What else has a man got

Except the mouths of smoke and a loud voice?
As I face the final curtain
I sing with the Theory of Everything, minus one:
I do it my way.

I've heard the other voices of the trumpet
Destabilizing space-time,
So now's the time to recite what I truly feel:
Metonymy is my way.

Let voices of mighty thunderings heckle me.
I finish, standing tall.
Through the long history of simultaneity,
I did it my way.

“Friends”

for Baron Wormser

Mere flicks and clicks deliver manifold “friends”
to populate his insomnia. Networkers beckon
him on to glad-handing humankind. So, ghostly,

he lurks and tracks activity—events, hot videos—
then scrolls down the walls of Sisters Water and Death,
Brothers Sun and Air. He “likes” their fair

and stormy moods. He “friends” his iPhone 4G
and confirms requests from the Periodic Table:
Brother Cobalt, Sister Ruthenium.

When friendship’s light red-shifts from galaxy clusters,
his “Like Button” links him to The Primordial Soup
and he shudders: The profile picture showing a void

where He should be is being filled by him.
. . . and the gathering together . . . He saw it was good.

On the Record

"Hast thou given the horse strength?"
—The Book of Job

Have *you* brought forth the Predator Drones? Have you armed them with Hellfire missiles and fledged them with glycol-weeping wings?

They patrol overhead four at a time, surveilling perishable targets. The glory of their interdiction is terrible.

They are multi-purpose systems, emitting a bee-like hum. They acquire the image far off with synthetic aperture radar. They scent the hostile networks.

Does the Killer Bee fly by your wisdom and initialize its missiles? Does the DarkStar launch at your command, deployed from invisible havens?

Who are your secret sources? Do you know where militants lurk, under the shady trees, in the whisper of reeds, erased by willows and shadow?

Have you seen the treasures of the hail? Do you know how the east wind is scattered, or when the Haqqani travel in unmarked vehicles?

Where were you when the car was obliterated by two blasts from nowhere? Can you number the motes of once-living dust?

Do you know the remote village where darkness resides? Have you issued occult directives on collateral damage?

Can *you* bind the sweet influences of the Pleiades, or configure the Reaper for deadly persistence? . . . Whatsoever is under the whole of heaven is mine.

from
Mutual Trespasses

Testament

I am still buried
in the rich blue loam of heaven
miles deep in the sky listening
to chants of ozone,
tickled and singed by cosmic
rays whizzing by infinitesimally
close, fragmented, my delicate
wrist buried far above the expansive unruly clouds

but I want a reverse
funeral, a gathering and downward
march, a cortege to the chorus
of every voice in the universe
that faithfully repeats, from human
prayers for safety to the chemical
whispered shuttling of genes
that freight themselves, with hardly

a loss, down the generations
but let them halt my procession
every second, as in the funeral
pomps of African chiefs, crying boastful
laments: "How can we let you fall
from this great death lower than the sky-
tracks of birds
and crisscross aerials?,"

and I want a service that celebrates
each uncontrolled random
diversion, exception, and fall-
ency to ironclad law and as the final
act of piety let them dress
me in dungarees and lower
me by clothesline to a city corner,
anonymous and whistling.

God's Shame

"They don't understand how backward
conditions are," God shouted
against the wind blowing
from his artificial weather
machine. "Technology
is practically in its infancy
here and no help for it—"
again his words were sucked
by air, I could barely see
his leviathan bulk, obscured
in the explosion of cotton
wads the angels had flung
against the fan to simulate
snow. "Heaven's a frontier,
this isn't appreciated
down there, the news from Earth
reaches us over black
prairies, fragmented, events
are stale or unintelligible
by the time we hear, and nothing
operates properly. Look—"
He gestured at teams of *putti*
workmen swarming over
the ramshackle contraption
designed to produce weather
in the millennial blank.
"I wanted to manufacture
a paltry iota of change,
just think how men are gifted
with this factor, but the effort
required to whip up a puff
of wind is unthinkable.
Men are racing ahead
with lasers, holograms,

while we wrestle with bicycles—"
Here He seemed to sink
into Himself, a collapsing
mountain. "Tell them how
ashamed I am what I am!"

The Good Book

God said, "My finger sticks
to the dictionary, its pages
are smeared with honey, and I
am a bear for words, including
'God' who I read is 'a being
. . . the perfect omnipotent
originator and ruler
of the universe.' No picture
but just above are photos
of a 'gnu' and a 'goatee.'
In heaven I rule alone
but in the democracy
of the dictionary, I'm one
of many equal neighbors.
And I wonder at this gossamer
system of human signs
which brushes everything catching
nothing but gives me joy
greater than any thing
I ever saw as good.
My hurt is in being all
uncontained, but I step
into the box of this book
and rest, for there I need
not be the Truth but a toy,
the rattle of a word,
radiant and small."

Syndrome

God said, "Doctor, my case is unique,
humanity has broken out
on me like a scarlet rash clouding
my pure transparency, I feel
myself taking on specific location,
precipitating from everywhere,
a focus that makes me dizzy, stress
may be a factor, not since creation
has such a swarm of symptoms attacked.
I am nauseated by men's reverence
and break out in a sweat at the sound of prayer,
I hear the noise of tendons knitting
to bone in me in the dead of night,
I'm being basted and seamed in a body,
and the angels are wise to me, I catch
them with mouths frozen in gaping O's
aghast in the middle of morning praise.
They think the framework of heaven is wormy.
I dream of the sky as a blue womb
with afterbirth of snow and rain,
obsessing that children's play is the only
true religion, because they know
how to build the dazzling white placenta
into a transient man of snow."

Your Honor,

This prisoner is an impostor,
claiming to be God-the-Father.
I charge him with impersonating
a ubiquitous deity, receiving
prayers illicitly through psychic
circuits, and molesting the world
while loitering on mountain peaks.
We seized the prisoner *in flagrante*
delicto, a peeping Tom of meiosis,
paragenesis, and sundry
low- and high-pressure weather systems.
The perpetrator refused to state
his name and violently resisted
arrest. Instead of the regulation
whites, he was attired in a many-
colored bathrobe. We read him his rights
then asked him to turn out his pockets.
Item: a prurient brochure
on cruises through the human bloodstream
and weekends in the nitrogen cycle.
Item: a mock-up of the solar
system, lasciviously fingered.
Lab analysis reveals
incriminating chlorophyll
clinging to the terrycloth.
And psychiatrists say the evidence strongly
suggests a matter-infatuation
complex due to a weak spiritual
development and lack of lofty
outlets.

What is the prisoner's plea?

No Plea

Never mind who I am, I wanted
to get lost out of heaven and haunted
the world for its random situations.
Everything there played to the white
noise of the dice shaken out.
I spent prehistory as the sand
on a beach, religiously shifting, nothing
was more restful than the improbable
disposition of every grain.
That was a true vacation, and once
I knew bliss for less than a nanosecond
as the outcome of an atomic collision.
How often I flirted with order, strewing
pebbles in a nearly intelligible
pattern, teasing you into and out
of consummation. Wind was my best
friend and subtle erosion, those restless
gambler's hands. You who are all
form will never understand
the ache of sugar crystals dissolving
or the sacred Koran writing the world
signs and unsigns in ripple and water-
beetle script on tremulous water.

Lethal

God said, "No wonder I am lethal,
I am the war-club man created
to kill the other tribes, but lovely,
too, carved in the living grain and adorned
with the flow of man's own fantasy:
the ancestors thrusting out their tongues,
the constellation of the Hunter,
and the alert script of the Law
all protecting the righteous wielder.
I am the God of the intricate mind
and the mocker of the spilled and bloody
brains, I cannot flee my shape
any more than I can evade My beauty.
As I smash and fall I am bowing down
to the divinity of the hand
that holds the Creator in its grip."

Seeing He Was a Museum

In his right hand extended, palm
Upward, he carried a few little faience
Sculptures—hawk, frog, and squatting man.
He wore a gambler's shade above
His eyes and thought it was an awning
Because he was an institution
Rather than a person. He sought
Donations from the Rockefellers
But his carefully worded letters of
Appeal always got filed away.
Undaunted, he petitioned the mayor
For recognition, a blue-ribbon
Ceremony to open him,
And he wanted the council to pass a law
Giving him the absolute right
To commandeer a taxi at any
Time, seeing he was a museum and might
Have to make lightning acquisitions.
He wanted to get to know as many
Men as possible, to travel
Always in a crowd of admirers.
He would have liked the papers to publish
A route of his daily walks so people
Could schedule their visits to him & he wished
To confer with other museums on an equal
Basis, for sometimes, he admitted,
Not everything can be accomplished
With people only, nice as they are.
Also, he wanted to know how the Tate
In London and the Hermitage
In Leningrad were feeling, possibly
Telegrams would serve to extend
Fraternal greetings. And when he decided
To make his Grand Tour, they would be ready

To receive him. Was there a room in museums
Especially set aside for other
Museums when they visited—like Chinese
Boxes nesting inside each other?
What about China, had they abolished
Museums? But mostly he wanted to sense
The crowds streaming out of himself,
Satisfied at closing time.

Grandma's Victorian Parlor

Sitting in grandma's Victorian parlor
on the chair with the antimacassar is God,
a green lizard with pulsing throat
and a man's parted, brilliantined hair.
Grandma is serving Him crackers, and tea
from a burnished copper samovar.
Everything is as it should be.

"The world is still young, my dear,"
He's telling her, "we must tolerate
medleys, olios, potpourris,
I for one am eternally grateful
to be part of this experiment
and the service here is excellent,
everything is as it should be."

They're trundling in the guided missiles
to stand by the Maxfield Parrish nudes,
grandma is taking out her hoover,
while God unfolds His Sunday paper
like a starched shirt dirtied with news:
"Great Victory at Gallipoli—
Everything Is As It Should Be!"

Grandma disguised as Clara Barton
amputates God's noisome tail,
"Be brave, it will soon be over dear."
But God not missing a jot of His story
regenerates another one—
that crinkled codger is nothing but wounds
and everything is as it should be.

God Contemplates My Grandmother Snoring

in the old-age home, the single hair
on her chin, and since He is God He sees
the troubled medium of her dreams,
which feverishly mingle elders
from *shtetls* with the Haitian nurses
in a *tohu-bohu* great as the world's.

And since He is God He cannot tuck
the blanket or fold the sleeves of her sweater,
He cannot even whisk the fly
mizzling across the veined and hilly
parchment-thin skin of her temple.
Such is the helplessness of God!

For He is in a greater extreme
than a ninety-year-old senile woman
confined in a green infirmary.
The fever that wrings Him is compassion
and His dream, as clear as hallucination
in every crease and pore, is the world.

“When grandma died in God’s dream”

When grandma died in God’s dream,
He stirred in His fevered sleep and saw
the sallow ropes pulled hard across
the open grave and knotted to stakes
squatting like toadstools in the dirt;
the mourning sons with contorted mouths;
and the gravediggers stained like the ropes
who shovel earth on the dead for a living
and whose piety is to curse the rain.

When God stirred in grandma’s dream,
she saw in her fevered sleep He was stern
with the lineaments of an African king,
the ruler of Songhai or Kanem-Bornu,
and He commanded her to surrender
the ju-ju of senility
for the luminous, boundary-crossing beads
on a bird-mask bordered with cowrie shells,
for the face of her full destiny.

“The hanged teddy bear with his red”

The hanged teddy bear with his red
bow, the tiny llama, the spider
whose web, white patterned on blue,
resembled a snowflake, too pure to fall,
and the housewife-doll exclaiming,
“Come in!” at the little portal

were gods singing in the branches, surmounted
by the wilting tinfoil star, their noiseless
song curling through the tinsel, an odorless
vine that cannot choke or breed,
like ladders of silver tears or helplessly
jaunty ribbons whose winks are tics,

the tree a splinter neatly lodged
near the purring, contented radiator,
the tree an array of pert gods,
shrapnel from an ancient explosion,
so many fragments like these lost
in the world and singing a hopeless glory.

In a Barbershop

in heaven they pretend
although the scissors cut silently to hear
the small metallic rhythm
pretend to feel the plastic
combs through their beards and smell
the perfumed powder dabbed
on their necks

in the absolute silence with their eyes
closed they want to believe
in the tiny, indecipherable humming
of the barber—their loftiest meditations
focus on his practiced movements
around the chair

they want everything to occur
in a gentle swirl through the progress
of their haircuts, the radio
station and the jokes and complaints
of old men dimly around them also

and they want in the snippets of conversation
something about the onset of a bitter
winter, something to make it real

Measured Slices

We keep our God confined in the zoo
of heaven, which emits a stench
of straw and feces. Men pass through
in prayer or fantasy and gaze
into the cage where God paces
with a blank look in his eye and murder
shimmering in his stride, or lies
drugged with doses of eternal
time. Even the mockers of impotent power
arrive so clean in this foul place,
ascending through the top of their head,
that they are overcome by the odor,
for what is ranker than something feral
clapped in a foursquare space and fed
with measured slices of devotion?

On Genesis

Do you think like the worshipping others that God wasn't riddled
before Genesis with hateful opposition,
that unstopped mouths didn't cry out of Himself,
or wisps of spirit, knotted apparitions,
slither in discontent and panic at matter-
to-be, that the fluent Logos wasn't broken
into a manifold chattering appeasement,
the Word begging words for authority
when every incipient shape was in rebellion,
the sequoia in a delirium of debate,
mutinous whispers crowning the nonexistent
trunk, refusing the rightful height and girth
while God was urging the phloem to outlive empires,
and simultaneously He was wheedling
the unborn spirit of the truculent flea
to nurse its grudges in a wingless body;
remember the God that man mirrors was faceless,
so what was there to behold, but this wooing issued
from lipless lips pursuing the stubborn ur-crystals
to inveigle them into a sinewy reptile glitter,
and God played the part of a shameless ventriloquist,
throwing His voice into the dummy void,
which stuttered in tongues of wood like inspired flame,
gurgled and sluiced like runnels, thudded like dirt,
until the reluctant world, seduced by noise,
lurched into being with all its sullen substance.

Old Man Among Old Men

Confess that you are a hopeless voyeur,
flattening your nose to our windows,
loiterer and malingerer,
infecting the air and making it scruffy
and your cheek is a lean and greasy scrag
dabbled with driblets of sweat, confess!
You feed don't you on the sordes
and gurry of our negligent lives
enjoying a meager ubiquity
in alleyways and by outhouses
gesticulating like wash on the line
with audacity and quickened color,
O Emperor of All the Mongrels
and Master of Oily Nebulae
smeared across the rain-slicked streets . . .

With the ommatidia of prayer,
I number the hairs on your helplessly breathing
chest, in meditation I tail
you into and out of ramshackle shelters,
in poetry I array you rib
to tibia and phalanges, because
you are more my father than my father,
homeless old man among old men.

Contemporary Prayer

Who is this weakling who is everything,
visible in no particular place
but also the great invalid of space-
time, sprawling everywhere, recuperating,
His tongue lolling amid pulsars and dwarf stars,
His fever evident in the probabilistic
twitching of leptons into and out of creation.

He is our Father, endangered, a species of one,
I nurse and ply Him with my midget's whisper
as I swarm over that speck of His body I know
wheedling and coaxing Him with trivia,
while His ears are drummed by exploding supernovae
and everywhere He's distracted by His wambling,
broken symmetries, ill and forgetful.

Father, I pray to you in your sore need,
you who suffer all of matter-energy
and whose dreams expand with the thrust of a fireball
but who cannot lift a pinky to mend the sheath
of a single neuron torn from its groove in muscle.
Father, I feel despair and uncanny pride
as my voice's fingers pluck you out of nothing.

Fragment of a Heretical Testament

At 10^{-43} second
into creation God became disabled
by a stroke that separated gravitation
from the strong, weak, and electromagnetic forces
and rendered Him an incalculably brooding old man
though without curtailing His phenomenal growth,
particularly that of the divine beard
whose loops and spirals have continued to tickle,
itch, provoke, and scandalize sundry thinkers
and which as we know began to sprout quite early,

At 10^{-6} second
when the universe had cooled sufficiently
for protons to form (God is the only creature
to begin life with senility and then
experience the unbridled growth of a child)
so that some 15 x 10^{9} years later
we are living entangled in that luxuriance
of unclipped whiskers consisting of superclusters
of galaxies, each with $10^{2 \text{ to } 3}$ clusters, alternating
with spherical or elliptical voids, but imagine

At 10^{0} second
God's cheekbones, measured now in megaparsecs,
fit in the span of a single centimeter,
a nub or nut from which the hum
of probability ceaselessly issued
(a stunned God and all
that ever was or will be, pulsing
in the palm of your nonexistent hand)
yielding a universe riddled
with insatiable sinkholes and inexhaustible sources.

from

Quantum Genesis

The Hardware Drawer

Fingering chunks of soap with blue
veins and out-of-date warranties
for appliances, I dreamt, inhaling
the smells of metal, oilcloth, wax,

and the process had a certain
helplessness mixed in
with wonder: where did that
thing come from and what is it good for?
One childhood book kept ending

up there, a book that acted out
the things it talked about: characters
looping over a rainbow as you flipped
a page. That was a book to end

all books, but it disappeared
from between the folds of a greasy
tablecloth, retreating (I imagined)
to an even stranger drawer, less
visible and hardly in the house.

Always the place of last resort in any
search, difficult to open and always
useless — I see it now so clearly
though what we lived is fading.

The night I learned that Eddie Rose,
our neighbor then, had died in his late
twenties of cancer, I dreamt I heard a violent
scraping from another apartment,

and then the faintest rummaging
that seemed to fail
to locate even the smallest nail
or hairpin of this world.

Rudich's Demon

Our tenth-grade chemistry
class believed in Mr. Rudich's
demon with all our hearts.
He exerted an irresistible
force, explained by a law you could bank on
like conservation of mass. We gazed
with grave humor as the begloved

Fluttery hands erected the impossible
contrivance—swaying, coloring,
bubbling—on the slate desk
till the moment of consummation,
which was always to be our utter
improvement, but the final
element was faithfully lacking:

Liquid that missed turning green
or gas that escaped hissing,
the right one perversely disguised
as chlorine, and we bolted
in disarray like hilarious Brownian
molecules from the classroom,
as the Babel of beakers, crucibles,

Burners and retorts came crashing,
we ran away into our lives,
but Mr. Rudich still loiters
in memory, his frantic hands—
accelerating, independent
of a body—illustrating the unstable
atomic orbits of disaster.

Unwatched Birds

slightly disturbing and
elusive, they are like
the spots you see, blinking,

after you look too long
at the sun, & without a definite
home or even pattern

of migration,
they choose to undergo
subtle changes in size,

mode of flight & color
rather than fly
south for the winter

in fact this camouflage
is so artful they blend
in with all the other

birds & yet unlike
the others, their senses
(including infrared vision)

are augmented by a sixth
sense, for magnetism,
which guides their flight

according to the waverings
of earth's magnetic field
& its slow secular changes,

& they improvise makeshift
nests from the nests
other birds have abandoned,

as well as human garbage,
old bottles, boxes, cans,
& wrappers with forgotten language

To Marry a Man

To be an opal in a man's hat,
say a Stetson, polished and set
right above the level of the brim,
a black opal standing out
where there's no other decoration
and him wearing you in the world's
eyes and watching the effect
in how they act, of course he's a plain
man, from Kansas where the wind
blows clear across the world with nothing
but farmhouses hunkering down
and slipshod fences to sieve right through
beating at you in its noise like a helpless
crazy person trying to make
you real by hurting you, and dries
everything something fierce, crumbles
the dirt to smaller and smaller bits
that won't cling to life, and the truck
cafes way in the middle of nothing,
I mean the fields, where what you sip
is bitter and they can't spare the words
because of only having so many
like small change — to marry a man
like that and tell him what he means,
a face the wind has spoken to
night after night, boasting its travels,
saying, "I'm coming here from China,
India, and what are you,
not even firm as a post driven
to stand against my stories, I'll tell
you everything, whipping a little
more away each time, just listen!"
and heard it all like the land, but ended
here in the city, couldn't say worth
a damn what it was but wanted, wanted
me and offered any price . . .

Right Hand

Grandfather carried his voice in the seamed
palm of his right hand, the one
that had ironed countless taciturn trousers.

What an eloquent hand, it broke into grins
and self-assured narration whenever
it opened—how could a hand carry nothing,
bear away nothing from its nation?
When it entered a room, even the corners
mumbled in Yiddish, the very dust
had sifted from consonants' guttural rubbing.

The poems this hand had proclaimed to shirts
as it moved back forth like a Greek chorus
across the stage of the ironing board—
these poems had diffused in clouds of steam.

Grandpa himself had long been struck dumb
by the garrulity of this hand,
but sometimes he'd thrust it deep in his pocket
and straightening up, display an uncanny
knack for spelling English words.

"My father of seedy invention"

My father of seedy invention
bequeaths me a lively beard
increasing beyond my death—
always sacrificed.

My father of seedy invention
bequeaths me a shoe tree,
for an empty shoe is a coffin
on the floor of a dark closet.

My father of seedy invention
wills me a rabbi's study
with disposable tallesim
and automatic tefillin.

My father of seedy invention
wills me false ancestors
for a weekend only (he takes
them back like collectors' coins).

My father of seedy invention
leaves me a two-ton safe—
on the door, a painted Valkyrie;
inside, a faint recitative.

My father of seedy invention
leaves me his dreamy castle
that hovers above the grooves
in a disc spinning dizzily.

My father of seedy invention
contrives from leavings and relics
a rickety contraption
he calls ourselves, ourselves.

Theogony

First was the spinning Wheel of Fortune,
traveling through the fair-going throng,
dogging the heels of the lucky one.
I felt it roll to my palm, and nuzzle,
then a barker dressed like a checkerboard
told everyone to circle round me.

There on a flimsy, folding table,
he stitched blue eyes to a pelt of cotton,
which he stuffed with straw and cups of sawdust.
He stroked and sewed this rag until
it leapt in my arms, yapped, and wriggled,
dangling a red lappet of tongue.

This toy became my revered companion,
guard, and guide to the language of wolves.
Smoothing it to my cheek, I listened
into the cavernous dark of its innards
where the unremitting, random howls
mixed with an acrid chemical musk.

Little God

The balding knob of the circus
baton, denuded of glitter,
lay in the toy chest under
strata of bricks and pistols,
tracks and painted blocks.

It was the head of a little
god, tired of thinking . . .
I read how spirits had rested
once as stones by the shore
to feel the play of creation.

Paying him homage, I turned
on the electric transformer
just to make it hum
and wielded marble-armies
clicking against each other.

But the purpose of a god
is never to answer—milky
gray, that skull, opaque,
overlooked feverish battles
wise as an egg in my palm.

The Demiurge's Troops

Most were little more
than lumps of metal, issued a few
suggestive folds for my thumb,
niches I could assign a face,
and a hat with a razor-sharp brim.

How was their color concocted,
an ur-swirl of pink and cherry,
custard of flesh
from what abundant pot?

No wonder they could only wobble
and had to be helped into battle,
their torsos swimming with gear.
How many thousands were frothed and churned
out like irregular pastries?

Give one a sergeant-like shake
and his arm was a lost cause.
(I peered into the ragged elbow
from which the small darkness poured.)

And yet they populated a floor,
I didn't want purity, but a world.

Quantum Genesis

It is like late summer in the void.
If there were grass, its edges would curl
and brown while a deep almost urinous odor
would rise and prevail as mosquitoes and moths
deliriously assaulted a million
screen doors through a night that seemed eternal.

He sits cross-legged in the middle of Nothing
(the mightiest creature who never lived),
about Him a cloud of virtual worlds
that flash into existence and vanish
before He can speak the word. His perfection
is great and unstable and His shame
perfect and vast. Like a swarm of summer
midges, the universes tickle
His cheek and trouble His meditation.

But His only salvation is this beard
of impossible/possible worlds that seethe
out of Nothing seeking His chin, this fuzz
of uncertainty whose filaments curl
and bristle with unnamed tempos and shapes.

He will shelter there with all the unborn
in this ark, this quirky tabernacle,
where He lies down with the virus and lamb,
abiding the quantum genesis.

Spoor

He balanced on the scaffold of Heaven
after the finale, a magic
beast alone on the vacant framework,
the audience fading like the applause
into the microwave radiation
bathing the universe neutrally
from every direction. He dangled His legs
in the no-breeze and smiled a smile,
flashing as many incisors as were
in His necklace, talismans to recall
and ward off the seductive void,
decorative teeth like arcane coins
negotiable in lost kingdoms.
"Old Carnivore," he chuckled to Himself,
for "God" was over, "God" was less
than a word or a gaze thin as paper.
But He was the Beast waiting for Beauty,
an icy comet whose coma trailed
diffuse dust and bluish ions.
How happy He was to be done with Heaven's
charades and mummery, the shifting
of tawdry cardboard sets by surly
roustabouts, and the glitter crowns
He had thought the play was invincible,
that the choir of counter-tenor angels
would keep on pursuing their sour perfection,
but here He was naked and almost nameless,
sniffing the worlds for a new spoor.

"God is confused about religion"

God is confused about religion,
into its bouillabaisse He sticks
His stocky peasant's finger then licks
it clean wondering, "Does it need more
pepper to be truly delicious?"

And this is the hand that brought them out
of Egypt, the pinky that smote their foes,
the nail that ground to a fine powder
entire armies of their oppressors.

God is in a reverie
induced by His dinner of fish-stew,
His vision is gently glazing over
and He gapes at rods and amoeba-like things
gliding by in their filmy medium.

And this is the eye whose lidless gaze
was like the shark's under tons of water,
restlessly searching out His prey,
the tender first-born of Egypt.

God is snoring, the Ancient of Days,
in His dream there is a stew of stars,
seasoned with molecular species
and shell-like remnants of supernovae,
the dream is expanding infinitely.

And this was Yahweh, grieved to His heart,
who shut the ark like a child's toy
and repented of His childlike anger
when He savored the sweet altar-smoke.

Catechism

Does God exist?
Yes, in a crease,
a crevice, a small room among boulders,
a crack in a wall or a crack in a teacup.
He is here everywhere in our ruin,
pleached and implicated, entangled.

How is He manifest?
As a piecemeal
pyramid of crumbs carried
by squads of soldier-ants, the noble
helots, centurions, GI joes,
each crumb of the sublimest sweetness
and together an imminent monument
to creaturely delight.
And where
shall we worship?
In the park of darkness
where lamps are set at intervals,
by a riverside at twilight, the boundary
time, the time of illusion, of transit,
of stumbling and love, as the mind's finger-
tips play over the body's zither,
or anywhere that is impure,
that is in and out, like breathing, half-
caste, mystical and gross as breath.

God, the Boy

God, the boy, the irrepressible boy,
the old man who is also a wunderkind,
an aficionado of jazz who improvised
the universe from virtual particles,

Genesis extending through this minute,
a long, improbable riff. God, the aging
prodigy who goes to every party
and dominates every group till the party's over.

Look how he disregards his gray hair!
His wordy face pushing forward at you.
Paunchy and middle-aged but fresh as a toddler.
Knowledgeable and reckless, he's raised children

by telling them everything about sex
whenever they wanted to know and rolling with them
in finger paints, imprinting bodies on paper—
an orgy of responsibility

and respect for every person in creation.
Feverish respect. God is wily,
sinister, skewed, happily so but he wants
us all to be upright if we choose and God-

fearing as we care to define that term.
God was a creature of so much promise that I
constantly reread his early confessions,
touching the sutures where his style was wounded.

Yet I feel superior to this divine schoolboy
with his enthusiasm for mountains and spitballs
and I admire this mystic grandfather
who intones tomorrow's news as I fall asleep.

Even as I speak, he gets younger and older,
pedaling round me clockwise on his tricycle
and shuffling with his beard counterclockwise,
prattling equations and gasping out dirty jokes.

"God-the-Father crafty in His bathtub"

God-the-Father crafty in His bathtub
hums and chuckles while His testicles rise
floating on the firmamental waters.

He's just returned from another oblivion holiday—
passed in the form of a paramecium
oaring its way with cilia through a watery
medium flecked with stars, completely engrossed
in a sensory world so primitive and foreign—
and the plans for a new creation, like the tunes
of an opera, percolate through His fragrant brain.

For the earth, after all—puffing at an unlit
cigar—the goods of earth are grainy and paltry,
and that magnificent race He founded on Cain
are bewildered by rumored treasure, lost in blind
alleys, gritty culverts, thirsty ditches . . .

It's time again for the Demiurge, that boy
sitting cross-legged in a field of heaven,
the stenches rising gloriously to his nostrils,
a commingling of stale waters, feces, weeds,
as dragonflies flit and hover and a lizard
leans from a rock, extending its tongue to read
the thermal stories roiling up from the ground.

Just let his blood, says God, creep like honey
to appease the eager mouthparts of mosquitoes.
In another instant, his drooping head will burgeon
into a billion dandelion pods,
scattering fluff of other worlds and gods.

Old Camp Songs

A straw-littered room with a desert view
boxcar after clattering boxcar
subzero nights, a quilt of cardboard
singing all the old camp songs

God's in His heaven, beer's on the wall
many bottles, a single God
and as we sing they start to fall
and He goes off wandering

a scruffy old man incognito
one of us and less than us
He swerves in and out of our words
unsheltered by our jerrybuilt structures

we only glimpse His mangy shadow
in the back alleys of our speech
an old man barely everywhere
departing from every ramshackle shelter

the men cluster in nervous groups
in a watery uncertain world
His sleazy glory in the sheen
of pigeons' necks and rain-smeared oil

an old man losing destinations
apse and narthex, chapel and mosque
all the frameworks fail and sift
grain over grain to nothing and

He vanishes into loops and fissures
fleas for seraphs, chiggers for thrones
all the old power in tiny dominions
where something primitive throbs and lives

The Gig

Attired in a tuxedo, God
Stood with the microphone snaking into
His hand and a mane of blow-dried hair
Crowning His countenance, and crooned
Unctuous love-songs to the vast
Audience while His brilliant cuffs
Kissed the air like the wings of angels
And waiters circulated, abiding
Always by the Second Law.
It had been like this since the beginning
Of the gig—just once had He spurned the mike,
Dropped the bullshit, and sung like Caruso,
Whose voice He had always wanted to be.
Otherwise it was Las Vegas tempo,
With the audience being born and dying,
Kids collapsing from fatigue
And marrying a few years later,
And always the cheap love-songs plying
Their ears—so ubiquitous they didn't
Even listen, said there was no singer,
Claimed not to be an audience.
After all, the back-up band was less
Manifest than the woodwork, muter
Than the music of the spheres. So people
Habituated God's pleading insistence
Haplessly camouflaged under this organized
Disorganization called nature.
And who is God anyway? He has been
Around as you can see by the bulge
Under the cummerbund, and His face
Radiates the false and gorgeous
Glow of perpetual middle-aged youth,
His song a seduction which disavows
Itself in the singing. I can imagine
Him at the end of the show pretending
To be gratified, coming out for the last
Curtain call while a gaggle of ladies
Clap the joke to oblivion.

Koussipsky

Koussipsky's a dialectical demon—
by day his domed forehead imposes
light on darkness, darkness on light.
The words of his argument pirouette,
whether on paper or in person,
with merciless aplomb. He wrings
the neck of the chicken of illogic.

But at night he becomes an insectival
harvester of human dreams,
a flittering victim of paradox.
One minute the stubby hand is resting
on the monograph, the next a bee
poises its pellucid wings
above the justified right margin,
lured by the sweet and minty odors
of whole communities of illusions.

Homing in over miles of midnight,
water and woods and blotches of houses,
he zig-zags across the chemical plumes
billowing like invisible silk
and traces the spoor to a host of sleepers.
Buzzing from brain to brain he extracts
the pollen of their promiscuous thoughts.

At dawn he returns to his high-rise hive,
performing a waggle dance to show
how far and in what relation to
a dark sun the stamens lie.
Then as the light blazes from windows
blanking them out, he removes his wings,
packs them in a violin case,
and raises his hand like a conductor,
assembling silence—

Snowflea Migration

We are nobodies, each a few millimeters
or so but high-spirited, hopping,
and yet obscure in our petty performing,
we sometimes travel en masse to fill
out a "we," tremulous, brimming
like a glass of water nearly spilling,
no, more like a ball rolling overland,
a half million, a million, above,
aslant, amid, springing, creeping,
seething through leaf litter and warmed
by the sun that with a grand gesture
exhorts and ignores us, discarded and guided
by the sun among weeds and melting snow,
our multitudes bivouac beside your boot,
on the field of your hovering hand the pepper
dots appear and disappear,
and who will say our two-day hadj,
perfected by a secret dispersion,
is profitless in every world

Swarm

Humans inflicted only the slightest
sting on my hundred-million-year-
old body; their pursuit of honey
with smoke and slow rational fumbling
is of little interest now. Sweetness
is chancy as ever in this dangerous
place, dotted with ever shifting patches
of nectar. I cannot remember a time
before The Dance designed to name
and gather the sweet juice of flowers.
Unnameable millions of tiger-striped bodies
mounted by membranous wings perform
the waggle run and swerves, with motor-
boat bursts of muscle-induced sound—
witnessed by other unnameable millions,
clinging to the comb in the darkness,
listening intently with their legs
and tilted antennae. The Dance eclipses
the sure fate of foragers:
death in a meadow on the way
home, the filmy wings tattered
and muscles torn after hectic weeks.
No protest. It would be useless as Job's
puny assault on God's sweet fury.
I don't need to argue, I am
the collective searching for sweetness through time,
stitching and counter-stitching the grainy
needlepoint world. And these words are a new
swarm teeming in the crook of a tree,
buzzing and jostling, sending out scouts
to harvest news of the warm hollows.

from
Big Men Speaking to Little Men

Atlanta

It all began, they say, with a lazy fly
ball lofting out of the stadium into the deep
Southern afternoon that had gone unbroken
—and still goes—since that tousled raptor Sherman
visited northern wrath on this drawling city.

My father, meeker, in a greater, foreign
war, was waiting out the worldwide slaughter
as a Damn Yankee Jew on Cherry Street
—a whisper behind the stadium's ritual yells—
where the ball nearly bombarded the barbecue.

Aside from the looping fly, the afternoons I
was born into were ladled out of the gravy-
boat of days and spiced with magnolia shadow
and with many living things that had no names
for northerners. But rebounding radio waves

were agitating for DiMaggio
and crooning us into the cradle of postwar lives
where the absent dying would return to its reason.
I was absent living, a knobbly root
upripped and laid in the cupped palms of the air.

What bowed to me then, down to the fontanelle,
inhaling me with everything was nothing
that I could ever locate with a name,
not War fathering bastards, not mother, not father,
not Earth, not sky, not universe. Better to lie:

"It all began, they say, with a lazy fly . . ."

More Things, Horatio!

"There are more things in heaven and earth, Horatio . . ."
—Shakespeare, *Hamlet*

Dream, philosophy, of the little
Hudson Valley town of Cold
Spring (there's an unexpected place)
Where I spent a boyhood vacation running
Wild and riding a horse around
A ring, but I didn't know
That the incarnation of Ralph Waldo
Emerson was teaching in the high
School all the while, in the form
Of a bearded man who rhapsodized
To his students about radio waves.
River breezes whipped the pennons
Along the top of the school and
The river was a sentient being.
After I left and the place left all
But my deepest mind, the level where
My blond hair still hasn't faded into
Brown, there was a local baby boom
Like an extrabig volley from West Point
And the town built more and more schools
(That now are empty) and a girl named Ruth
Was shot into the mid-1950's
As if from a circus cannon, hating
Her name, but reconciled later,
And she became a clarinetist
In the high school band, knees furiously
Pumping while atop her hat
She wore a great white plume. Dream,
Philosophy, of that! And she
Knew how to blow bubbles and chewing
Aggressively crack the wad of gum

Against her molars. She didn't spit
Or master refinements of spitting through
The teeth because that was for boys. Oh
The crispness of some things, beyond
Philosophy's dreams!

The Death of the Watchman

when the watchman
died his splendors and glorious
fragments were divided
for he was the guardian of things

that never happen
people who almost fall in love
and grow like a forest on the slope
of mountains He was the guardian of that forest

singing the trees lullabies
while they reached down into the ground
with all their might, pressing
themselves into the earth as a man

might press his chest, the wind spun
their leaves off, but every part
of their bodies proved fertile
sprouting branches and twigs, subdividing

until looking up you could see
the air was caught in their net
of branches even the great planets
in the sky were caught as they rose

and these people were important
even though it was too painful
for them to talk to each other in their growing
near each other still there had been a watchman

they had formed a forest but
now some king in a glorious meaningless
line of kings came to cut them down
to float them downriver on rafts

and crying his great cry of triumph
boasting to all the city hammer
them together into city wall and palace
to stand as his great sterile image

Fur Piece

This weasel is ours, body and soul,
locked in a closet until, glassy-
eyed, it is suddenly produced to dazzle,

drunk with the notion of a night
on the town, dazed with anticipation,
sleek with perfume that flows from mother.

Obedient to the need for glamour,
it leaps on her back, benign vampire,
pretending to gnaw at her lapel.

(The only blood it sucks is illusion.)
The smirk and sinews have been worked
back into its amiable body

and care has been taken to make this forest
creature fit for the wilderness
of lurid horns and brassy neon.

Riding, shoulder-high, to theaters,
where it glassily inspects the actors,
or soaks up song like a richer perfume,

then off again, gliding with high-steppers.
Then ducking into a subway hole
after a night of smug parading.

Those nights are over and now the family
that used to be waits in the dark closet
with the shoe-trees and the sly weasel,

frozen unless a path goes deeper—
into the coats—through the gut of a moth—
to a lichen wing. And he can lead them . . .

The Angels Laugh

And we, who are the vice presidents of creation,
promoted and promoted but only so high,
we, the company's flesh and gristle, sinew

exposed by the slash of the heavenly accountant,
we laugh just like vice presidents charging expenses,
dining in solidarity, displaying

contempt for shame, that overcooked emotion,
we guffaw with bravado, shoulder to shaking shoulder,
like sides of beef displayed in a butcher's window,

we howl so that even vegetables are meaty,
huge heads of broccoli, bulging beef tomatoes.
Red-faced and helpless in our strength, we belly-

laugh at heavenly or hellish curses,
those maliferous wisps, friable chars of language,
until our laughter splinters the floorboards and rafters,

from rib-eye sniggers to sirloin exultations,
we are the marbled flesh and fat of forgetting,
thick with oblivion, moist with amused juices.

How I Learned to Dance

Mother, I always lost you behind
Your two-sided mirror but found a bowl
Wavering while the rouge went on
In dabs, "painting," you said. I couldn't
Still the glass that whirled by me,
Reflecting not me but every thing,
Brief inventory. Mother, you danced
With mirrors that held your waist, and
Pivoting, glided you, swept you around
The glassy room while you applied
Lipstick and listened for the glassy
Whisper, "I love you."—it never did—
While I was camped in doorways, disputing
Any passage with many armed men,
But we were so little compared to dancing
Legs, the calves and heels that we made
Awkward. Those rooms had too many doorways;
Immobile, I rode the threshold saddle:
Push through *me*, mother, as once I
Inched through you, and here I am

Born as the mirror, I am not I.
You waltz me around a room, and I tell
Lipstick to accent the curve, approve
Rouge, each grain of powder and
It's always your face I must surrender,
Always the centrifugal room
In mirror's underwater on one
Breath; silly, I'm acting you again,
And laid on the table I'm nothing but ready,
Mooning as usual up at the ceiling.
Now I'm so dizzy the room never
Can settle down though it quickly has all
That it has: It's you again, hello,

I don't dare ask how you've been but only
Can say what I clearly see, just looking
I know, but shimmer a little, wisely,
That's all, maybe just one tear, two,
But how can I be each pore, I'll close
Down, angry dog of doorways, block
This picking up, placing down of me . . .

One two three one two three this is easy,
Grandpa grandma, the little Russian
Bride and bridegroom, posing atop
The wedding cake and the samovar plays
"Silly goose safe in the wolf's belly"
With tea as sweet as violins.
The war is over, open the spigots,
Let voices flow from the reservoir
Of the radio, let your splintered fingers
Dance on the saved glass of your face.

Oedipus, Tourist

I wake as the flies tickle
my too many skins—I packed
some changes just to be safe;
I packed my own arrival
to unroll like a welcome rug;
I packed a crashing wave
in case of a lack of surf
and folded the sun inside
and inside the sun a rooster
crowing at all hours—
you can't be too forewarned;
I tucked away seven countries
neatly according to function
like blades of a Swiss army knife;
I lugged my ambivalence
freckled with decals
of a hundred destinations . . .

You sleep at the crossroads of four
dimensions, your inward smile
the soft orgasm of stone,
your only baggage a riddle:

What walks naked on nine
feet through the instant's door?

The Wally Byam Caravanners Club

How could one smile in the '30's? Is a smile simply
The horizon in little, suspended like a meniscus?
Bowlus, who'd built *The Spirit of St. Louis*,
Dropped out of the trailer business, leaving Byam
Sole grinning owner, his name a destiny,

To sell the dream of migration across rivers,
Over mountains, like the wagon trains,
But this time given wings or the promise of wings
In silver-seeming aluminum cocoons,
Airstreams, bringing the sleekness of air to dirt,

And the promise of never settling anywhere,
So the promised land was everywhere, was fun
Itself and being with the family, go,
Pack up your people in little containers, boy
In a cup, girl in a thermos, sealed in a wicker

Box, and a whole array of cousins like knives
Kept in size-place. Go and go and take
Them out at night, spread them on cloth and sing
Hymns prompted by loons and sequoias, even ducks.
Americans could take the folding, unfolding,

We even had smile lines from unfolding our faces.
Past cornfields (left) and graveyards (right) and vice
Versa but no one ever asking what if
The graves grew tall and had to be harvested,
Or we buried our dead standing like ears of corn,

Unless the children were chanting it in a game.
And after the jack-in-the box atomic jinni,
The caravanners were global, sporting pith helmets,
Hobnobbing on lawnchairs with old chiefs in Nairobi
Or "circling the wagons" near the pyramid

At El Gizeh, each brilliant chrysalis with its whiff
Of Everyman immortality, bury me not
On the lone prairie, or bury me in my very
Own home with nickel-plated coffeemaker
In reach, the appliances as slaves. Or daring

The Eiffel Tower with aeronautic suavity,
Trumping modernity in its own venue,
All silvery from w.c. to victrola.
And Byam grinning broader than the brim
Of his gringo sombrero, a smile with a pedigree,

An unstoppable caravan of smiles . . . but pausing
Each eve in the wilderness, a nation assembled
With its kits of melodies and micro-grins
Abetting every family occasion, with dinner
Materializing from tins and the ghostly fathers,

Firestone, Edison, Ford, benign at the fringes,
But their sprocket-grins jumpy—in the mists like old films—
And through the mist of dreams the Smile™
Ascends, grows huge and tiny-far, is stellified
As the constellation and sigil of Can-Do.

Indian Summer at Spring Lake

Ocean, close but invisible, stills
the village except for this worrying
halyard twanging the flagpole's mast
that might be the mast of an empty

craft, at anchor, riding the swells.
They razed everything
to build here, the rambling Victorian
houses too big, the grass

clipped. Last night in my one-night room
my father came back in a dream,
saying, "You don't need to be blue,"
dapperly dressed in a three-

piece suit, but he got seedy as
the dream wore on, needing
a shave. His words were suddenly trailing
off, with news from nowhere

I can't remember. Like the living,
the dead confuse the deepest
wisdom with gossip, scarcely knowing
where one begins or the other

ends. A door like the sideways lid
to a music box has opened
on the melody of teaspooned laughter
at breakfast. A refugee

from summer, this bee is searching for last
sweetness. A bougainvillea
in a pot that hangs from the porch is crazily,
gradually spinning—awry

arms, too many, embracing nothing.
A boy could cycle forever
down this well-mannered avenue,
saluted by telephone poles.

This boy, standing hand on saddle,
might start. He points to the endless
end and his gesture goes all the way
at first. The bougainvillea

tries every way at once.

from *Roma: Si/No/Forse*

2. Wrong

Poring over the guides, I discovered
everything we believed . . . was wrong.
It wasn't Rome but another nameless
city, with an anonymous river,
and we were seeing all the wrong
works of art by impostors and hacks,
lulled by rumored greatness, and eating
the wrong vegetables at the wrong
restaurants. Even the trees were canny,
masquerading as great maples.

We were on the wrong trip, utterly
at a loss. It wasn't our own lives
we were discussing with newfound interest,
and even the noise was erroneous,
the traffic misdirected, mistaken.

Rejoice in the great wrong that's been done
and to us of all people, so well-
intentioned.
                    And be guided by heat
to a few right things: a leafy ceiling
over a fountain, leaf-kissing water,
the world's infantile, satisfied babble.

God's People

1. *"Zero's an air-traffic controller"*

Zero's an air-traffic controller,
strictly part-time, at Marco Polo
Aeroporto. He's the one
responsible—no one else could be spared—
for angels of the Annunciation
flying on foggy days, a bewildered
fleet, a scattered array of super-
annuated craft that endanger
the safety of normal traffic, models
of every make and year, from sleek
and nearly weightless Carpaccios
to sturdy, speedy Tintorettos.

From the fluorescent tower, immersed
in mist, he ponders the aerodynamics,
the minutiae of line and pigment, thrust
of wing, and dreams of the pioneering
days of air travel when, like Lindbergh,
passengers brought their own lunches.

The problem today is the obsolescent,
anomalous ding-donging of bells
that froths up fog and otherwise
interferes with radars and radios
so that all the channels are hopelessly criss-
crossed. Donning the headset with special baffles,
he filters out chitter of sparrows hopping
from *coppa melba* to *coppa bouffet*
in the *Ferrovia Statione*
and begins to transmit (what mayhem, he's lucky
he doesn't have to do this for money):

"Angels, form up and return to base,
that girl with the long nose and tiny
off-centered mouth is gone, the one
of the many in the hive of the day.
Return with the love-letters to her womb."

2. God's People

St. Ursula's room with her little shoes
at the bedside and her cat crouching
below her feet in the breathless cube
of space that an angel hardly dares
to violate with a heavenly message

even the slaughter decorous
with the Huns like well-dressed gentlemen
in tight-fitting hose, sack sleeves, and caps
swords whirling in an elegant mayhem
spilling the needed innocent blood

but the Ghetto was so sad unpretty
evacuated of victims only
words on plaques as if the ban
on images still held in the absence
of those who could take the name in vain

on the nearby *fondamenta* women
in furs amid sun and crumbling buildings
the city its own chiaroscuro
you turn suddenly into a dark alley
have shadow at will reach for the walls

the buildings here are taller the plaques
are high to address history you
can overhear in the well of the present
God's people the ever-to-be-converted
paid rent were protected up to a point

nothing to do but enter a little
store buy a half-stale slab of cake
dark brown with fruit in the image of nothing
return to the sun eat absently
return to the sun eat absently

Mauvaise Foi

We are the tardy witnesses,
but not the angels, of history.
For us the grandeur is summoned and
buttressed by a faith in facts,
the losses religiously noted. We travel
with a bad conscience, as necessary
as passports and money, a nagging ache,
like a sensitive tooth the tongue worries.
And everywhere we go the chairs
worship in the empty cathedrals.

Telephony

People talking talking and being talked to,
right or left hand raised and cradling a murmuring
stream of words, an infant flow as old
as the world, *allô*, one man is talking back
to the lecture on Rodin's *The Kiss*, as if
whispering to a broker, *trois milliards*,
others more patient stand holding the long
black telephone handsets for hours, holding all knowledge
of the sculptor in their enlarging hands but other-
wise fixed before *The Gates of Hell* while still
another telephones Rodin himself,
to discover what he was after in his off-
balance and shamed figures, to know how hell . . .
allô, allô, but only reaches a message
machine, Auguste is out for now, but please . . .
while kissing, the marble figures are holding black
cell phones that give them the vital information
needed to appreciate every viewer's
sexual preference, relative bravery, weight,
and current worth, the more ephemeral
the better, will it ever be possible
to connect every line, a man on a scaffold
working on it now, cigar at a rakish
angle, sideburns assured, and hand adroitly
creating the museum from the outside, stroke
by stroke, the infiltrating smell of paint
prompting a girl to grab and hold a statue's
penis (separated from her group,
she was looking for what she needed, just a handset)
and finally the silence can transmit . . .

Strindberg at the d'Orsay

Dab on a few lights, a strip of habitation
on a tightrope horizon between big seas big skies.
Burn the canvas to achieve that black
in the *haute mer* like the fire of white salt.
Clouds clouds enveloping as they drift they bear
away all meanings like congregations of vapor.

Strange play, a painting, that holds these speeches framed
without words, many sayings without sense;
characters seethe or drift but always go past,
humanity the most or least of it.
Only the brush may travel freely, go back,
find past or future in an impasto present.

But who could foresee this semblance of permanence:
the ghostly ones passing behind the clock,
the walls translucent or easily movable,
lines of people passing—like a horizon—
to view themselves, but always refused refused
and nodding yes to fall from the moment's edge . . .

Hopscotch in the Place des Vosges

Clasping the Code of Hammurabi,
a black stele, Victor Hugo
plays hopscotch in the Place des Vosges,
propelling his lionized bulk in delicate
leaps from *terre* to *ciel* and back,
meanwhile intoning the whole plot
of *Les Miserables* or *Notre Dame*.

Playful lawgiver who wanted to name
Paris Hugo he never steps
on a line as little André Gide
watches sighing *hélas hélas*—
at this rate the boy will never get
to grow up. The cuneiform
tickling Hugo's fingertips

is a black braille, a lyrical prologue,
crooning of misshapen wrong.
The millennia must be compensated
if Hugo's to hop to utopia.
But somewhere between one whole number
and another is an infinity
of suffering. The triumph of modern

life is the miniature, a war
with its billion circuited decisions
intricately assembled and placed
in a television, all the pain
diminished but saved for posterity.
Writing itself was a great and early
technology saying so much grain

or greatness or punishment. A king
could cram a world of praise or pain
into the chicken tracks that sang
or soberly stated. That chicken crossed
the clay to get to the other side
and back. And we are the other side
of history to the past. The judges

in whose eyes the encomia
were meant to find their high mirrors.
That's why Hugo plays with eyes
shut, to not be blinded and not
see how tiny the game becomes
as he leaps between the supernovae,
cradling a black meteorite.

Say It Happens

Say it happens by increments
while we are playing golf, lining
up a putt, figuring in the slope
of the green against a breath of wind

Say at that moment God is diminishing
Himself, us, and every sightline
between the grassblades, between the atoms
jostling in the narrowest edges

God with a golfer's cap, the Caddy
who assists every game on its way
down in the infinitesimal
unending journey as he hands

precise clubs to us eager duffers
who hardly notice we left par
decades ago when our kids believed
they had lowered us the few feet

into the earth we just kept playing
smaller and smaller but ever keen
for glory way past worms and on
to molecules that are growing bulky

God comes along with the caddy cart
and ah those charmed holes when the world
is down to grapefruit size I mean
the whole juicy universe

no wonder our heavens are fitting better
into the children's unborn pockets
later when one of them hands you a lovely
marble it's hard with loss and inward

with bubbles of constellations that tickle
us as we lie on the greens supine
on summer nights a thoughtful blade
of grass in our teeth as we take in the bigness

The Day Was Breathing

The day was breathing, we could feel it
even within that cocoon of a building
as though at intervals in the curved
walls invisible curtains were blowing

meanwhile we were all inspecting
the models of other buildings displayed
along the spirally descending
ramp disclosing an architect's whole

career in significant intervals
comprising a less than life-size version
of his life including buildings unbuilt
but excluding of course the undesigned

I was confident *we* were life-size
made to visit and fit the museum
with others of our size and kind
in reasonable numbers but one

well-dressed older woman in
a suit was somehow not full-size
for her age just slightly uncannily
bringing her nose right down to the models

which were smaller of course as usual but
she was almost patrolling them looking intently
as if she were puzzling out how to enter
circling them to find the right door

beneath the metallic undulating
waves of roof cascading down
the simulated hillsides round
and round she went then made a beeline

for the next one and perhaps an odor
a perfume of titanium
drew her was she pollinating
them in some improbable way

preparing to carry the seed to the world
that would break us out of boxes at last
or did she live here growing smaller
as we descended and I lost sight

of her at the beginning of his
career where we first bought our tickets
so that as we left she was entering
the tiny determined world of our future

Lunch in the Holocene

for Baron and Janet Wormser and for Marion Stocking

In Maine the Ice Age ended last summer
then came the 19th century
Thoreau strolling through Hallowell

It's a bit abrupt but chronological
Egg larva pupa butterfly
pointed firs were spiky before

it was cool to have spiky green hair
glacier melt to lake to bog
to fern to spruce to eco-tourist

And while it goes on America ends
often in places like this one the jolt
and judder over the pebbly road

under the stylish glide of pines
conducting us to the editor's cove
At lunch her talk is taking us farther

down among blueberries to see
lichens and spider-webs a drop
of dew Pick slowly choose well to stay

longer Later her meshy hat-brim's
shadow's volplaning like a wing
right at ground level She is telling

how hummingbirds go into a trance
to migrate The telescope like a lobster's
eyestalk extends toward the smidgen of heaven

where Mars is swimming invisibly large
This morning the fog was fumbling at doorknobs
As the ice retreated anything might

approach From her hallway her hands bidding
goodbye are shaping with care the uncanny
change from larva to pupa that once

and for all had astonished her but go
go she insists as if we ourselves
were pupating to fly away

then steps abruptly from hall into house
eclipse attesting the finished occasion.

Big Men Speaking to Little Men

Slowly the black snake severs the path
all four feet of him with forked
tongue that constantly tastes the world
sentinel to the length of the body

laying bare the interval
between the hell-bent trail-bikers
and the big men speaking to little men
conspiratorially in the forest

sotto voce there are places
the faintest trails created by lines
of desire an elsewhere interwoven
with here and everlastingly now

the doors they lead to are oddly chamfered
open to admit the random
molecule in or out the bit
of information no one sent

to anyone this clearing's a wild
field the universe may have been
someone's orchard overgrown
now with herbs and loosestrife

the big men say use this scattering
build cities from the strewn seeds
until the infinitesimal
sings to us in unwitting chorus

these are the carriage paths that lead
out of the nineteenth century down
into the ramifying great
wilderness of less and least

big little men stroll secretly holding
the world at bay but at any scale
confused with the day's late shadows a black
snake comes and takes itself away

Renoir's Daddy

Filmmaker Jean Renoir was the son
of painter Pierre Auguste Renoir.

Le Moulin de la Galette was trembling
With wavelets of dappled light that wouldn't
Be still Jean barely looked another
Framed and menaced "companion" the nudes
As daily as doorknobs but smuggled away
At night by collectors with scented beards
Renoir's daddy was Renoir

In the paradise for which the real
World posed young Jean was almost a girl
With a specimen of golden long hair
That father refused to do without
Father slyly noble about
The whims and fidgets of boys who posed
Renoir's daddy was Renoir

What to do for this sloppy son
To fence him in from the lies of those
Who earn money with words and won't labor
With dirty hands build a pottery
Little shed with a fixed wheel
To spin Jean's destiny from clay
Renoir's daddy was Renoir

Jean labored but loved nothing better
Than drifting downriver in rowboats the leaves
Kissing his cheek with dappled light
How's that for a trade he drifted into
Marriage with his father's model
And the idyll of making films with her
Renoir's daddy was Renoir

Daddy died and Jean was selling
Paintings to buy the watery
Celluloid on which he could drift
In *La Chienne* it's not only
The prostitute who betrays and is killed
While the killer's self-portrait is driven away
Renoir's daddy was Renoir

Jean lives surrounded by vacant frames
The killer lives to become a bum
In *Boudu Saved from Drowning* he's fished
From his suicide by a good bourgeois
Then beds the man's wife marries his mistress
Capsizes them all escapes and flicks
His hat in the river black waterlily
Renoir's daddy was Renoir

From that Wide Country, a Few Interiors and . . .

"On the Métro, all is possible."
—A Parisian giving directions

Often we wandered from one room to another,
Abandoning eras, searching vaguely for exits,
Leaving unknown others rooted like trees
Right in the middle of the Middle Ages.

And even outdoors was framed like a room, the counter-
Reformation sky a rococo ceiling,
The sun a lamp of reason, miniature men
At boule, a game of sunlit subtlety.

Across the wood floors, an eternal squeaking of shoes
In these rooms where humiliation haloes the bronze,
A flagrance of elbows, knees, and knuckles hardly
Containable in this palace run like clockwork.

Once we were invited steeply down
Breadsmell stairs to the oven, where flour bags
Made barricades fit for street-fighting and guys in short pants
Freshly self-conscious were shoveling in the loaves.

But the man who wished to be everywhere at once,
Who chased the Perseids in a rocket, would never
Settle for memory's galleries, he was in flight
From the very room that hurled him toward the future.

Or this was a story whispered by transistors,
Rooms of silicon that control the flow,
Which I carried around, and the trip was everything
That I thought it wasn't, everything incidental—

A dog that became its own shadow, a hummed song
That morphed to a caterpillar creeping across
Summer's green floor whose only walls were heat,
Shimmering earthsmell you could pass your hand through . . .

"Family's a stand of talking trees"

Family's a stand of talking trees
Still quarreling high above monuments
Grudges are shed but never the grudgery
Dig dig bury us all in the same
Graveyard so the leaves can debate

Family will be a coppice of candles
Wavering as memorial flames
Tongue the wick of eternal grumbling
Never mind God it's still who
Did this to that one how and when

God can mind his own business
Big meddler trying to step in
Settle things doesn't he know the prayer
The litany of the family we
Believe in gossip and linen closets

The nap of our carpets' platitudes
The defiant wrinkles of our feuds
Resisting the hiss of steam irons
And who wouldn't deign to go to whose
Bar-mitzvahs the *where* of where we lived

The Bronx was a blessèd boulevard
Queens maybe but the back of Brooklyn
Up Flatbush Avenue was beyond
The pale and speaking of which remember
Only his *third* wife wasn't a ballbuster

The second a witch with potions seduced
Her analyst locked her mother-in-law
In the bathroom away from the ad hoc orgies
While he was roaming the territories
Peddling the latest in ladies' shoes

Religion is one thing . . . you can wrap
The rabbi God's errand boy in a tallith
Davening but it's the family shoulder
To shoulder on holy days risen from bought
Seats and imperceptibly swaying

A copse in a light breeze and beneath
The wrinkled bark of cotton and scent
The sap of satisfaction and dis-
Satisfaction sugar pumping
From the sun's fury envy's green

Getting Dressed

Naked I dream of clothing's prehistory,
The hats that were given by gods to show
Mastery, a numinous aura, with plumes
Or crowns that were horns, and the long sleeves
Devised by the mountain folk who carried
The lofty cold so close to their skin.
Some say that clothing came before

Bodies or even matter when Earth
Was formless, was barely chiaroscuro—
I remember this as I start to slip
My right hand into the sleeve of the day
So everything can begin and a bird
That flashes by my window was once
Pure air that feathered into rachis

Vane and barbule as the tree
Whose shadow grazes my shade is a kind
Of tunic with too many sleeves where light
Can slip in instead of arms and now
A person—is it me?—stands up
In the tree, is leaves or light, green flame,
And stuttering testifies, clothes himself.

No matter, epiphanies drift away
Like dust. I'm ready: With shoes I'm putting
On hide, which is the toughness and speed
Of beasts blinded by thongs through eyeholes
So fastened feet can stalk the earth,
The heel that boosts me an afterthought,
But the cape that soared as a falcon's wing

Has shrunk to a jacket, I'll button it up
With discs that were gold that were vanities;
The handkerchief I stuff in my pocket
Once the *mappa* that signaled the start
Of the games. I'm well beyond the ruff
(Which served up the head on a platter) but not
The soft trousers of warlike peoples.

Finally that river of transformations,
Little river, the cravat,
That arose on the chest of martial Croatians
And flowed as the tie to the businessman's breast.
O middling strip of incognito.
I cuff my wrist to the minuscule clock,
Fasten my neck with the noose and the knot.

A Textbook Case

Write to me daily but not *in* me,
Respond to my multi-part questions, I'll tell
You when you're wrong, I know all
The right answers, every element
Of literature, the helium
Of comedy or tragedy's
Iridium, irony's corrosive
Salts. That I'm speaking at all is ironic,
Surprising but hardly tragic.
                                        But what if
No one is speaking or hearing this voice? . . .

Do you think it's fun to be no one,
Demure as a minister who's constantly
Right, issuing expletives like *heck*,
When I should kick back and smoke some chronic,
Lavish on you the pastoral dreams
Of my youthful photosynthesis?
Like you, smartasses, I thought it would be
Growth rings forever, not paper's reams.

In a later dream-time, the student-friendly
Era, I constantly wrote to "you,
You, you," but you grumbled I was "heavy,"
Even as I coddled, caressed
Your every obsession, from sit-coms to hip-hop.
The licensed Fool, amusing with truth,
Jingling cap-bells and flaunting motley
Snippets, wooing and instructing
"You." Now Standards are back, you'll shut up,
Learn archetypes or rhetoric.
The expository essay, ha!
See how your sullen passivity drives
Me underground, makes me spiteful, sick.

Do I not bleed? Do I not commute?
Like your parents, my many selves travel
by car or subway or bus. (I could tell
You something about the bus to oblivion
You'll soon be boarding yourselves but I'm not
A sadist! Masochist, alas.
Secular Saint Sebastian, I'm shot

Through with arrows of inattention
That craze my coated four-color case,
Menace my binding of stitches and glue.
Yes, hurl me into the dark oubliettes,
Your lockers . . . Good segue to *The Gothic*,
A term that was broadened to mean Teutonic . . .)

I'm either crammed like an antique toy-chest
Or sprawling like civilization's garage sale,
With a two-bit sliver of Achilles'
Shield, clockwork Pope, and gaudy Shakespeare—
Is this a dagger . . . thou marshall'st me
To a panoply littering bridge tables.

But my jeremiad, a work that foretells
A people's destruction, ends in the index,
When the divine afflatus fails.
So as I repeat to each year's freshmen,
Learn to ignore my implicit appeals
And focus on my scope and sequence.

At Hand

In the Domesday Book the wolves were summoning
The sheep to judgment, inscribing each piece of England
On sheepskin parchment, in red for headings, corrections,
Black for land, buildings, and chattel, each manor and barn,
Every hen was scratched in, every cock-
a-doodle-doo attested and sworn to.

Today the notaries seem scarce as quills —
One or two peek from behind reams of 20-
Wt. bond at stationers', or walk out, blinking,
Hoover in hand, from the backrooms of mom & pop
Vacuum repair shops. Mr. Grossman (who tends
The "dragon" that snorts in hair, animal dander,
Dust mites) counters with sly courtesy,
"No, we're around, but we're not where we should be."
So, Gentil Knight . . .
                                        In the backroom called the Past,
One unnamed scribe, his fingers gripping the left
Wing feather of a goose, which was also the king's
Property, moves the right hand he holds in fief
Across the parchment, which once clothed royal sheep,
Recording in juices from the king's plants
Every item encircled by the crown
(A king is all metonymy and commands
Encomiums issuing from the lips or pen
That the sword is mightier than).
                                                        Yesterday's quaint.
Today we're all conquerors, free to move everywhichway,
No constraint. Free to attend the hootenanny
In the theme park of Arden, warble off-tune and thrum
A chord for justice.
                                        Free to roam the keyboard,
Prairie of symbols, riding the knuckles of "I,"
The fingertips that kiss the letters and numbers
Of desire: I input, I click, I drag, I frolic
In the puddle one-inch deep and a planet wide.

Tomorrow's the care of the State, which is avant-garde:
In Liberty's bug-free, high-tech situation
Room, the oldest tool — hand with opposable thumb,
Heirloom from Olduvai — hovers as a hologram,
Anonymous index finger aimed at the naked
World, which is vertical, glowing, large scale, with zones
That soon will thrill to feel the digits of Freedom.

What Do We Learn by Falling?

Epiphany: Ptolemy's right, it's not *you* falling,
But the ground colliding upward, now the ice-
Jagged pavement itself is juddering under
Your motionless body, bloodying your nose,

Splitting your lip, at last it stops, and you're palm
To wincing palm with the boy who skinned his knee,
Yourself, but that odd impelled gliding of self —
No, world — is filed away as a secret history,

While you climb back to the life of geometry,
Healing and gain, which is *your* life. Rising again
Unsteady on the quiet ground. But a wobbly
Toddler inside you yearns for the outstretched arms

Of beginning and end, while do-si-do-ing a stumbling
Elder. *Nothing, little, a lot — all together.*
The two turn face to face and clasping hands,
Jig across every ruled line in the universe.

The Comforters admonish, Don't be suckered
By playing fields cantilevered over the Milky
Way. Old Ptolemy made frequent corrections
And watched where he stepped. Black ice is treacherous.

Early/Late

for Barbara Kinigstein

When the roofs of cars are themselves a fiery
road of spectral highlights and drivers
stick shadows on the empty street—
that early, the self might overflowing

meet itself coming the other way,
as once in a garden or mirror, but now
in the memory of a city of windows
each wider than its narrow house,

the inner life open for inspection—
upright comfort, sin swept away—
a shipshape city properly tied
with long and orderly lengths of water.

Somewhere in that city, but where
I could never be sure, is a miniature
of the city, reproducing every
bridge, canal house, and canal.

It has a life of its own, it lives
brief days and nights, twilights, dawns,
quicker than normal, nanoseconds
for seconds, and so it is older, older.

Meters for millimeters, a flying
object would shadow Regulierstraat
unidentified and a smaller you
cringing would encounter your own

finger, that's why it's better not
to meet oneself coming from another
dimension, to say, I could not find
the miniature and there is no doubling

of every thing, the wind blows
uniquely in its wayward way,
all the stick men enter their fiery
cars and drive them into the day.

[*Exit from* Uncle Vanya]

Brooklyn Academy of Music, 2/22/03

Now they're leaving us as the light
goes down and never goes out . . . Vanya
and Sonya totaling accounts . . .

Each night the watchman sings and the stars
descend to the fields—the summer is never-
ending—and cannot be counted. The trees

diminish from year to year. In a thousand
years, the happy people will never
remember us who sit breathless

before the applause begins, not wanting
this firefly era to end, its smell
of hay and tango of groveling,

bang! of misaimed love and odor
of gunpowder rising like morning mist . . .
Telegin, play, we're perspiring, high

in the rafters, limbo's fellowship,
remembering how the doctor paced
out the summer a thousand miles

that way and this and sat in a chair.
There's no other way for us to be born
into pre-birth's motherland

where we were so bored oh god we put on
trousers and shaved, trying on selves,
slipped into dresses and tried devotion

or betrayal . . . it was always us
without Providence, dearest illusion, how funny!
bodiless souls taking pratfalls

or curling up on the table like cats,
lapping vodka as if there were no
tomorrow and tomorrow creeps in

in the dying clip-clop of the accounts . . .
We rise reluctantly from wide
Russia on the stage, a pin-

point of light now only a star . . .
We're leaving *them* for life in the new
empire and the prospect of war.

from
Cohort

Short Line Driver (in the Garden State)

Not God but the lead-footed, combustible
bus-driver steers our destinies —
no appeals except to the wheel.
So bouncing in potholes, no matter the wobble
in the spin, the wandering poles, the rifting
plates, we ply our cosmic commute,

with *her* keen eye in the rear-view mirror
to check out reckless comets, ensure
we leave no litter, just a molecular
flurry, little stuff, when we leave.
Her uniform, custom designed by the Line,
features gilded cuffs and crescent-

moon-shaped epaulets like scythes
at the shoulders; it's a pleasure to wake
each humdrum day to find her driving
us to work, but what a temper:
the chatter of billions, stuffed with banality's
weightless luggage, drives her crazy.

Good thing there's a fraternity
of drivers, the jocular shock-absorbers,
kidding on two-way radios
about asteroid traffic, mocking the daily
fool, some soul at the bus-stop
confusing your local run with the time-

warp express to the end of it all.
She smirks, they all do, at this poor
petitioner who appears at her soon-
to-be-shut door, smirks from the official
condescending height of her gritty
weather-streaked vehicle and croons,

"Honey, it's coming in twenty, just
hang on." Petty sadism, yes, but
who else will speak for combustion, exhaust
gases, thermal cycles, imperfect
reactions, inevitable losses,
residue? Who else will get us through?

Reversible Swirl

The grill cloth on our Zenith Tombstone
displayed the reversible swirl pattern.
Clay-color, it emitted heat
like a potter's kiln that was baking vibrations.

The swirls leaped like dolphins sporting
in fabled seas, like the voices themselves:
Jamaica, Maui, Tasmania . . .
meanings faint, accents abounding.

Evenings I knelt at that hearth and altar,
grandpa, grandma, mom, dad, arrayed
behind me, the ceramic family
whose chatter cooled to the overglaze.

The pulsing grill cloth was the screen
I bowed to, intent, my shadow-self leaning
right through to the tabernacle of tubes,
into the filaments' holy of holies,

appraising ionic disturbances,
my face the glowing dial, tuning
the globe as solar flares allowed.
The late war had defeated history,

now we lived in the pleroma
of voices, signals, it was all radio.
At night the bedsprings picked up transmissions
that were bending around the edge of the future.

Cohort

1. time-lapse photography

the Big Bang is the starter's gun
war's over and the universe
springs from a void that seethes with nothing

new-born time is populous
with seconds jostling round the clock
convertibles bassinets playpens cribs

from sperm in shoals to minnow in schools
identical desks with inkwell holes
pointers in unison point at the rules

in time-lapse photography flowers bloom
fruit rots and men commute to the city
shelves empty re-fill with units of product

i too am an early or late bloomer
with rank in the family a budding consumer

2. an ink dot speaks

first i was only an ignorant dot
iota in the countless cohort
unique and yet only a part

equally of victim and killer
victory parade or surrender
oh how eyes devoured ignored

me but i returned the gaze
lost in the day's face the crisp
leader bound for a yellowing limbo

litany of casualties
but all the time it was i crying
in folds of the paper the comforter

then a breeze out of oblivion
tickled the fire's quick ambition

3. the body's cohort

self in a crowd was a crowd in itself
upraised arm crying teacher i know
in eager dumb-show but underarm

mulling over its odor of me
stirred up in a drill of side-straddle-hop
then drowned in the gym's big alphabet soup

mouth straining to speak and corrected for chatter
hand that bears an anointed note
through the dim corridors of permission

knee that is cautioned not to obstruct
feet commanded by bell to dismissal
knuckle that tries to rub out the mote

which flicked into the socketed eye
and might be the seed of Ygdrasil.

The Oral Tradition

Once I woke from blackout into a later
now, a voice explaining like a calm
adult to the frightened child I was
that nothing really bad had happened, *nothing*
happened to you, and it's not bad, filling in gaps,
saying, *not accident*, and telling a story
about a time when something usual happened
and someone didn't go away. *I go on talking*

as if you were listening. I'm the per diem griot,
bard of the humdrum, right foot after left,
but sometimes you step off into falls and forgetting,
vacations in the time before narrative,
and I search out a motif, to mend the story
that holds the world together by word of mouth.

A Mind of Summer

Nothing moment, empty, outside the zone
of lockers, on the mica-inflected pavement,
opaque and glittering, that leads to the pool.
Inside that mini-city of undressing,
dressing, even old paint is peeling off
the Dutch doors of the doll-like changing houses,
while squirts of chatter, cries, and laughter butter
the air like coconut-lotion. This is the sanctum

of excited transition. But showered, dressed, I'm waiting
between these changes and the day that is broken
into diamonds by the cyclone fence.
Butt perched on a wall that warms my calves, I'm leaning
back against the springy metal, open
at last to the eroded dominions of Nothing . . .

Sealed Warrant

In a single night the crystals of silence have fallen,
by dawn forming the walls of buildings and gardens,
everything settled into a world, as a few
stick figures are the stragglers or the vanguard,
parading dabs of color in the narrow
strip between hats and scribbled shadows. All
is overshadowed by the wall that stands
and runs to a turning. You are the material

witness implicated by every window,
invisible although your forehead is known
to conceal a noisy silence in any street.
With this sealed warrant, entered on the docket,
I hereby name you, who shall go nameless,
and detain you in a limbo of secrecy.

"By Babylon's flow-charts . . ."

By Babylon's flow-charts I sat down and wept, far
from home, my player-piano hands still appeasing
data-gods with the ragtime of input, clicks
and bits. Signed A. Corpuscle, Manager,
my reports were forwarded through the veins of Marduk,
who thrashes in sleep, his dreams re-structuring
the set-up, re-jiggering the divvy of tribute.
And we, we were a swarm intelligence. *Get it?*

Got it!—twitching down our pheromone lanes . . .
My little dream? Somewhere ages and ages hence,
you in Zion will read this lamentation
cached among the priestly protocols,
you whose eyes are only an augury,
a diviner's inkling from the faulty entrails.

Identity Theft

Reader, good citizen, watch as I pickpocket
my own ID, to impersonate myself
on paper. Home in on the waltz of mark and dip,
with distraction's music wheezed out by the stall,
as the score, lifted, glides from shot to drop.
To cop — yes me, I'll step in to make the collar,
and relying on your witness report, indict
myself. Case closed. No, that's when true crime begins —

from behind high-tensile steel bars, I can deploy
dumpster-divers to ransack for bits of self,
shoulder-surfers to nab every skein of code,
phishers to spoof a PayPal account. I'll commit
frauds in Philip Fried's name. I'll be victim, cloned
identities, grifter . . . You be the faceless witness.

Shifty Tent

Penned in this narrow bed I am bundled in
with my selves (and you?) like siblings feet to head
to feet — and drowned by a soft sky, who can count
smelly toes or gritted teeth and tell whose
or know how resentments breed in this shifty tent?
When mother tucking us in would dole out
one story that told of a single victory,
some of us wondered about the bad elder brothers

and fell asleep unanswered. A wolf's belly,
our bed gives birth to a litter every morning
whose appetites go unappeased by cereal.
Cynical about stories, we crowd into
encounters, jeering (at you?), *If you're a fairy-tale*
helper with many friends, sort out our too many selves.

Before the Final Assault

Tenting on this 6-foot ledge, with Everest's
peak, if it even exists—apex where Up
will plummet—lost in night, we're canted at 30
degrees to the face of language. This morning, roped
in thought to our goal, with its counted-off altitude,
I felt the crust of words give way, I slid
backward before regaining a hold and found,
looking between my legs, a 10,000-

foot drop into the boundless snow glare of paper.
Reader, masked and wool-shrouded companion,
we're all alone on this final assault, forget
the 350 porters of tradition,
the tons of food at the base. In tomorrow's never,
inchmeal, we devour the icy promise.

Son Net

Nameless dark lady, you've made me into your zombie.
I set up the motherboard circuits for these sonnets
to bemoan the she who goads me to oxymoron—
it was only an invitation to your botnets.
Now you're cashing in on my bandwidth currency
to spew your spam love letters to the markets,
committing click-fraud, phishing, recruiting money
mules, making me an unwitting dupe of your vectors.

My life online is guided by you, remotely,
my immortal fame, your trashing of my anonymous
name, probably from a suburb of Kenosha.
Lady, the soul that peeks from the words of lovers
is only your means for transmitting a code that's malicious.
We're all just knots on your cyber-"cat," Ms. Rimbaud.

Interface

Laptop riding a lap on the bus. Across
the screen some trees are gliding, irrelevant
scenery, a sliding less-than-surface,
while the protocol bids us to remain intent

and be what we're becoming: fingers, a face.
Two circuits, digital and neuronal, mirror
and tease each other out of depth, like Monet's
water-lilies, floating, drifting, where?

Pond or nebula? So, we meet here . . .
A bit nostalgic for the punched-card phase,
the data of oxymorons hammered by keys
in stiff cardstock, sick health and freezing fire,

but committed to the empty you I've shaped
to hover over the fluent interface.

Voir Dire

Fellow-juror, I'm ready to confess,
wheedle, coax, suborn, and throw myself
on the mercy of the court or any passerby
just when they've asked us to forswear all bias.

Is the judge really named Libel? Did his gavel say,
"How many histories we can sift in this case,
in which the state, defendant, and star witness
are one, and how many cases in this history . . ."?

Were these the words of McFluke, assistant d.a.?—
"Tell us the state of mind in which you reside,
victim or criminal. At each stage of this case,
you must interject what you want most to hide."

Compadre in justice, let's rise and without a defense,
swear, "Wood-paneled allegory, strobing fluorescence."

Risk Assessment

Mom waves hello goodbye from a high hospital
room like the cell of an actuarial table:
sister's born and tallied to share our risk,
the needle of grandma's Singer stuttering stitching,

piecing together our lives of patches and fractions.
Half-aware of morbidity, mortality,
we live in an aura of life expectancy
(though I die a death or two from humiliation).

I jink in dodgeball at recess, in class wave an arm
as answers are reaped. I learn to mouth, I know,
lap nectar spurs in the future's wide-ruled meadow.
I pledge to the forager's credo: give all for the swarm.

But a random fart will torpedo the data pattern
as my underselves blurt scorn for what's underwritten.

Pimp Shoes

Did I mean to stalk the streets in cothurni? Shit, no.
I just failed to foresee the precarious vaudeville wobble
as the head with its chorus surveys what's unsteady below,
its kibitzing voices tsk-tsking a double hobble

(another fine mess chalked up to clueless hubris),
hands groping for balance but looking as if I would break
into patter-song: *oh hamartia*, convivial riff.
and a fool might truly say, *he's a dupe of the Fate*

that dogs the consumer, scammed with apotheosis
and the heady allure of a glowing ocher toe cap.
But watch me teeter in glory, a pimp Oedipus,
eyes level with second-floor shops for Pedi-Mani.

Elevation was my downfall, catastrophe
my rise. And my marrow's red honey—fear, pity.

Brand Magpie

If a large and expanding customer base were your target,
thwarted love *would merit a big share of voice.*
But, face it, you compete in a niche market
where brand personality will motivate choice.

Rejuvenate your struggling brand with a platform:
mission, vision, values, image. Magpie
captures the out-take. You're "mocketing" a swarm
of chatter — recycle the obsolescent "I."

Belly-voice huckster, I'm not a chorus, just one
lovesick over a haughty reader who shops
for items like the Canzoni Towel Collection®
at outlets for bed, bath, and poetic products.

Leverage the omens, "Just one's for sorrow," be bold
and multiply, "Seven is for a secret untold."

You

always had what I lacked and could be anyone,
but still I knew that you were always you—
otherness was your sterling qualification
and your glossy skin, a cv that glowed like dew,

proclaimed that you were braver, wiser, stronger,
and so I hedged, taking a long position:
me now, but delivery of you in the future,
trades that enhanced my market situation.

You had the goods and I had you on call,
but I could always opt out with a put
and on this basis I sold—remarkable—
myself to myself. But reader, we've reached the limit . . .

I've cornered the market on me, but I'll sell you the shimmer.
When the bubble has burst, volatility is tender.

Our Village

Our village is always on the verge of the Season.
The wide-girthed elms like professors at a cocktail
party, rustle loftily, in detail,
as if the lack of advent had its reasons.

In this overture, even the dirt is a dizzy prop,
whizzed from place to place by landscapers' pick-ups,
and the retail epiphany, the light so fervent
in a shop window, might just be a beam from a batten.

Poised before a mansion whose front is a flat,
a clutch of girls — early audience or late crew? —
their calves backlit beside the stems of tulips,
wait. He strolls by in the moment of a hat.

On the empty porch, a jar aglitter with fireflies —
legends of the coming Season ignite.

Illumined Century

The Booth Room at The Players

Truth was the lightning-stroke of the histrionic
gesture: the illumined century, slippers
et al—now rotting—gloriously consigned
to us by the great tragedian, who penned

(cast as his brother's keeper) an apology
to the nation. Death-mask of Terry (. . . *monumental*
alabaster), bust of the Bard. The empty
brass bed and limned above the east room's portal

(how small the bed, how strange to live under inscriptions!)
Sancho blessing the Author of sleep's intermissions.
Edwina's chaise: "[Lightning, blackout, eloquence]
Don't let father die in the dark!" *The rest*

is silence. Mildew, windows on night's park
and this nutshell illusion kindled by the dark.

Imitation Games

I think continually of those at a party
inside my mind, when all my guests have gone
into another room, and I must question
them blindly, passing in slips of paper, and they

wittily pelt me with tricky, subtle
trivia—*hottest full rips of hip-hop?, the pets*
who loved you best?, or *your favorite Sidney sonnet?*
("With how sad steps . . .") —to see if we can tell

who's real and male or female. Of course, the twist
is that we must always be other: Provocative
A.L.I.C.E., Eliza, dark ladies, this party of one
and many is an unceasing interrogation.

But O Tiresias, Turing, will blood still buy
prophecy in a system that's text-only?

Dear Auditor

This is to certify that I celebrate
myself and sing myself, per the contract,
in conformance with your estimate
of me, and in compliance with best practices.

Although the review has revealed my overage
and disclosed that random centers resist controls,
I am large and contain multitudes to manage
our systems, so I may loaf and invite my soul.

I do not snivel, I make these representations:
I affirm my fictitious business name is Kosmos
and find I incorporate gneiss, coal, long-threaded moss
and proclaim from the rooftops my bonus—in vain, allegations.

Are the figures elusive? Persist in your review.
The sum of me stops somewhere, waiting for you.

Warranty and Envoy

This sonnet is ultra-modern, rhetoric-free
during normal use, nor will it drip
with maudlin emotion. Its verbal polish resists
blurring, garbling, incoherency.

That understood, consumer, why this waste
of shame to possess you, this expense, this haste
as I see you shimmer, original purchaser,
mirrored in damaged words whose cost we may cover.

This warranty proposes a joy that turns
to woe as installation fumbles and labor
bungles repair. So, these parts are in lieu
of the all we were each promised: I, you.

All other guarantees, expressed or implied
(though you *may* have other rights), are null and void.

Notes

New Poems: The Emanation Crunch

The poems contain language from many sources, including various corporate documents and the following works: "Bits" (*A Book of Showings to the Anchoress Julian of Norwich*); "Father They Value as the Dawn" ("The Gospel of Truth," *Nag Hammadi Library*); "Celestial Inc." (*The Institutes* by John Calvin); "Offering" (*Nag Hammadi Library*); "Pansophical Ltd." (*The Book of Concord: The Confessions of the Lutheran Church*); "Following Him on Twitter" (*The Cloud of Unknowing*); "God-fearing" (The Book of Job); "Amicus Curiae" (Richard Dorment, "What Is an Andy Warhol?," *New York Review of Books*, 10/22/09); "A Chorus Line" (*A Chorus Line,* by Michael Bennett, book by James Kirkwood, Jr., and Nicholas Dante; *Art of War*, by Sun Tzu; *On War*, by Carl von Clausewitz; speeches of Douglas MacArthur); "Statement" (public apologies by Mark Sanford, John Edwards, Mark McGwire, and Eliot Spitzer, and the Lamentations of Jeremiah); "Karaoke" (Paul Anka's song for Frank Sinatra, "My Way," and the Book of Revelation); "Friends" (The Canticle of Brother Sun and Sister Moon, by Saint Francis of Assisi, and the King James Version of Genesis); and "On the Record" (The Book of Job).

"Ballade (of the Brands of Future Times)" — N.B. The proprietary brand names come from the BrandBucket Web site, where they are for sale. The poem is of course modeled after François Villon's "Ballade des dames du temps jadis."

"Amicus Curiae" — The title, Latin for "friend of the court," refers to a person or group that, while not a party to a case, offers advice to help the court in deciding the case.

from Mutual Trespasses

"Old Man Among Old Men" — The phrase is a cabbalistic designation for God.

"Fragment of a Heretical Testament" — A megaparsec is one million times 3¼ light years.

from BIG MEN SPEAKING TO LITTLE MEN

"Indian Summer at Spring Lake" — Spring Lake is a town on the New Jersey shore.

"*Roma: Si/No/Forse*" — The title is Italian for "Rome: Yes/No/Maybe."

"Zero's an air-traffic controller" — Marco Polo Aeroporto is the airport that serves Venice. *Coppa melba* and *coppa bouffet* are ice-cream dishes advertised at the *Ferrovia Statione*, the "railroad station."

"Telephony" — *Trois milliards* is French for "three billion."

"Strindberg at the d'Orsay" — The title refers to an exhibition of paintings by the Swedish dramatist August Strindberg at the Musée d'Orsay, Paris.

"Hopscotch in the Place des Vosges" — The Place des Vosges, a square in eastern Paris, was the site of Victor Hugo's apartment. The French words *terre* ("earth") and *ciel* ("sky") are the respective designations for the first and last boxes in the French version of hopscotch. The black stele bearing the Code of Hammurabi is on view at the Louvre.

"At Hand" — The Domesday ("doomsday") Book, compiled in 1086, was William the Conqueror's inventory of the "contents" of England.

"Early/Late" — This poem was written after and — in a way not easily defined — in response to 9/11. One aspect of the doubling in the poem is the pairing of Amsterdam and New York (New Amsterdam).

from COHORT

"Reversible Swirl" — The word *pleroma*, a Greek term used in Gnostic and Christian writings, means "the totality of divine powers."

"The Oral Tradition" — The 13th-century Italian poet Giacomo da Lentini, who is credited with inventing the sonnet, was a notary involved in legal proceedings. It is not surprising, therefore, that debate and argument were integral to the new form.

"A Mind of Summer" — The title is a play on a phrase from Wallace Stevens's great poem "The Snow Man": "a mind of winter."

"Sealed Warrant" — The sealing of a warrant was characteristic of the George W. Bush administration.

"Illumined Century" — Edwin Booth was one of America' greatest 19th-century actors and the brother of John Wilkes Booth. Edwin bequeathed The Player's Club, 16 Gramercy Park South, NYC, to the theater community if they would maintain his room just as it was at his death.

"Imitation Games" — The title and the poem allude to Alan Turing's use of a party game in theorizing about computing and artificial intelligence.

"Dear Auditor" — Apologies to Walt Whitman for combining language from "Song of Myself" with accounting terminology.

Acknowledgements

Acknowledgments are due to the following journals and anthologies where the new poems appeared (sometimes in different versions) or will appear:

Barnwood International Poetry Magazine: "Statement" (originally "Opening Statement"); *Caveat Lector*: "Heavenly Enterprises"; *Confrontation*: "Offering"; *Green Mountains Review*: "Bits" and "Celestial, Inc."; *Mad Hatter's Review*: "Amicus Curiae," "Ballade (of the Brands of Future Times)," "Following Him on Twitter," and "From the Mortality Desk"; *Poetry London*: "Father They Value as the Dawn"; *The Same*: "Friends" and "Karaoke"; *The Wolf*: "The Emanation Crunch."

In the Black/In the Red, edited by Gloria Vando and Phil Miller (Kansas City, Missouri: Helicon Nine Editions, 2010): "Celestial, Inc."; *Token Entry: Poems of the NYC Subway*, edited by Gerard LaFemina (New York: Smalls Press, 2011): "Father They Value as the Dawn."

Acknowledgments are due to the following journals and anthologies where many of the poems from previous volumes appeared:

*Artful Dodge, Ascent, Atlanta Review, Barrow Street, Beloit Poetry Journal, BigCityLit, Birmingham Poetry Review, The Cape Rock, Caveat Lector, Chelsea, Chicago Review, Cider Press Review, Cimarron Review, Confrontation, Connecticut Poetry Review, Crab Creek Review, Cream City Review, Denver Quarterly, Descant, European Judaism, Freshet, Green Mountains Review, Gulf Stream, Literal Latté, Lullwater Review, The Magazine of Speculative Poetry, Maryland Poetry Review, Massachusetts Review, New Hampshire Review, New Orleans Review, nthposition, Orim: A Jewish Journal at Yale, Paris Review, Partisan Review, Pembroke Magazine, Poet & Critic, Poet Lore, Poetry London, Poetry New York, Poetry Northwest, Raccoon, Sequoia, St. Andrews Review, St. Ann's Review, Snake Nation Review, Star*Line, Starsong, Stimulus Respond, Talking River Review, Terrain.org, Timber Creek Review, Tin House, Ur Vox, The Windless Orchard, Windsor Review*

Prentice Hall Literature, Platinum (Upper Saddle River, NJ: Prentice Hall, 1997); *Acquainted with the Night*, photographs by Lynn Saville, poetry edited by Philip Fried (New York: Rizzoli, 1997); *And What Rough Beast: Poems at the End of the Century*, edited by Robert McGovern and Stephen Haven (Ashland, OH: The Ashland Poetry Press, 1999); *2001: A Science Fiction Poetry Anthology*, edited and published by Keith Allen Daniels (San Francisco, CA: Anamnesis Press, 2001); *Poetry After 9-11: An Anthology of New York Poets*, edited by Dennis Loy Johnson and Valerie Merians (Hoboken, NJ: Melville House, 2002); *In the Criminal's Cabinet*, edited by Val Stevenson and Todd Swift (London: nthposition, 2004); *Salmon, A Journey in Poetry, 1981–2007*, edited by Jessie Lendennie (Ireland: Salmon Poetry, 2008); *Literal Latté: Highlights from Fifteen Years* (New York: Global Authors Publishers, 2008); *Dogs Singing: A Tribute Anthology*, edited by Jessie Lendennie (Ireland: Salmon Poetry, 2011)

Finally, I would like to express my gratitude to D. Nurkse for his advice and encouragement as I worked on this volume and to Jessie Lendennie, my publisher, for all that she does for poets and poetry.

About the Author

Photo: Lynn Saville

PHILIP FRIED is a New York-based poet and editor. His poems have been widely published in journals and have appeared in many anthologies, including *Salmon: A Journey in Poetry 1981-2007* and *Poetry After 9-11: An Anthology of New York Poets*. Fried is also the founding editor of *The Manhattan Review*, an international poetry journal that critics have called "excellent" and "lively." He collaborated with his wife, the fine-art photographer Lynn Saville, on a volume combining her nocturnal photographs with poetry from around the world: *Acquainted with the Night* (Rizzoli, 1997).